Ethan Allen

A LIFE OF ADVENTURE

Ethan Allen

◆───

A LIFE OF ADVENTURE

Michael T. Hahn

THE NEW ENGLAND PRESS
Shelburne, Vermont

Cover painting by Ron Himler
Printed in the United States of America

For additional copies of this book or for a catalog
of our other titles, please write:

The New England Press
P.O. Box 575
Shelburne, VT 05482

Library of Congress Cataloging-in-Publication Data

Hahn, Michael, 1953–
    Ethan Allen: a life of adventure / Michael Hahn.
      p. cm.
    Includes bibliographical references (p.) and index.
    ISBN 1-881535-09-6 : $10.95
      1. Allen, Ethan, 1738–1789 — Juvenile literature. 2. Soldiers-
-United States — Biography — Juvenile literature. 3. Vermont-
-Militia — Biography — Juvenile literature. 4. Vermont — History-
-Revolution, 1775–1783 — Juvenile literature. [1. Allen, Ethan,
1738–1789. 2. Soldiers. 3. Vermont — History — To 1791.] I. Title.
E207.A4H17 1994
974.3'03 — dc20   94-9242
                                      CIP
                                        AC

Contents

Introduction

THIS IS A BIOGRAPHY of Ethan Allen, a man large in both size and spirit. Ethan was a strong-willed pioneer who played a large role in the formation of Vermont and the birth of the United States of America. He was a complex man—a skilled and respected military strategist, businessman, and author, he was also a rowdy, hard-drinking man-about-town who shocked and angered many people with his opinions and actions.

Ethan Allen used his leadership abilities to make sure that Vermont became a separate state instead of part of New York, New Hampshire, or Massachusetts. He also led men into battle to fight the British in the Revolutionary War. His business sense helped him to make a fortune in real estate. He used his convincing writing style to express his views of the world, many of which were very controversial at the time.

The story of Ethan Allen's life is important to anyone who is interested in American history, but it is much more than a factual account of a significant person. The tale of Ethan Allen's deeds provides a fascinating glimpse of a unique person who changed the world through the force of his character.

1

◆

Ethan's Youth

Ethan Allen was born in Litchfield, Connecticut, in January 1737, the first of eight children of Joseph Allen and Mary Baker Allen. All eight of the Allen children survived childhood—a rare feat in those days of widespread diseases and little knowledge about how to cure them. Like most of his brothers and sisters, Ethan had a name that came from the Bible; Ethan is an old Hebrew name that means "strength" or "firmness." This name certainly fit him because Ethan later became well known both for his physical strength and for his strong convictions. When he was still growing up near the frontier, Ethan earned a reputation as a tough hunter who could run on a deer's track all day.

Shortly after Ethan was born, his parents decided to move away from Litchfield, following the lure of the frontier as their ancestors had done since arriving in New England over a century before. Pioneers usually moved west to find uncrowded spaces, but the area west of Litchfield was blocked

3

by the mighty colony of New York. Most of the land there was already owned by wealthy landlords, so Joseph and Mary traveled north with their young son to the settlement of Cornwall, in the northwestern corner of Connecticut. Ethan grew up in Cornwall, near the Housatonic River, and all of his brothers and sisters were born there.

All the Allen children were baptized in the Congregational Church, although their father was not a very religious man. Joseph was inspired by love of the land more than by any church sermon. He taught his children to respect the land and to try to become property owners—a lesson they learned well.

Like most rural New England boys of the 1700s, the young Ethan wore leather breeches. He went bare-legged during the warmer months and added leggings in the winter. He had wide shoes with round toes, a homespun shirt, a fur hat, and a coarse coat. He wore the same clothes every day except when he went to church or on some other formal occasion, when he wore a long tailcoat and a cocked hat whose brim turned up on three sides.

Joseph Allen sometimes worked as a surveyor. He set the route for a road from Cornwall to Litchfield, and for another road south from Cornwall to Kent. When his father was traveling to do these jobs, young Ethan had to work even harder than he usually did to help support his family. He cut firewood—tough labor that developed his growing muscles. He caught fish for his family, and he hunted and trapped game for meat and valuable pelts. When he was a teenager, Ethan carried grain to the mill in Woodbury over a blazed trail for twenty-five miles. This was quite an accomplishment for a youth, but Ethan was big and strong and more than equal to the task.

Although he worked hard outside, Ethan's education was not neglected. His parents taught him to read, and their preacher and a few educated neighbors helped with his tutoring. Ethan had read every book in town by the time he was a teenager, but there weren't many books in Cornwall then. Much of his early reading was from the Bible and Plutarch's *Lives*. The boy wanted to learn more, and his father eventually agreed that the family could get by without him for a while, so Ethan was sent northwest to study with the Reverend Jonathan Lee in Salisbury. There he learned arithmetic, logic, Greek, Latin, rhetoric, and other subjects. Ethan was a good student and was preparing to attend Yale College, but that plan was ruined when Joseph Allen died suddenly in 1755 at age forty-seven. Ethan returned to Cornwall to help bury his father in the back pasture and to assume the responsibilities of the man of the family.

The English colonists in America had been fighting against the French for years in an off-and-on series of conflicts known as the French and Indian Wars. This was actually a battle for possession of North America. In 1755, eighteen-year-old Ethan was too busy with farm chores and other domestic duties to get involved with the military. During the summer of 1757, however, when he was twenty, Ethan joined a company of settlers at Salisbury to fight in the regiment of Colonel Ebenezer Marsh. The regiment marched toward Lake George to help defend Fort William Henry, but they were too late. While they were still marching toward the fort, scouts brought back reports that it had been captured by France's Marquis de Montcalm. The regiment turned around and went home, so Ethan didn't see any military action on that trip. But he had thoroughly enjoyed the thrilling journey through the untamed country north of Massachusetts. Long after he returned to Cornwall, thoughts of that northern wilderness tempted the young woodsman, drawing him toward his destiny.

2

◆

Ethan the Businessman

ETHAN STAYED IN CORNWALL for five more years to take care of
his family. He ran the farm, bought and sold land, cut wood,
fished, hunted, and trapped. In those days most New England men spent their time at similar pursuits.

The only backwoods industry then was the making of
potash, a white salt that was used to make glass and soap.
Potash was highly valued in Europe, and New Englanders
could trade it for sugar, rum, tea, needles, tobacco, gunpowder, and other goods they needed. To make potash, you
would run water through wood ashes until a dark liquid
called lye was produced. Then you would boil the lye until
it was completely water free and only a dry gray residue remained. To make a ton of potash, you needed four hundred
and fifty bushels of ashes, but there was an abundance of
wood in New England in those days, and the more wood
you burned to boil the lye, the more ashes you produced to
make more lye. The iron pots that the settlers used to boil

the lye were hard to come by, however, because there was a shortage of iron kettles of all types in North America.

When Ethan was twenty-five years old, he decided that his brothers Heman, Heber, Zimri, Levi, and Ira, along with his sisters Lydia and Lucy, could run the farm without him, so he went to Salisbury to get involved in the iron business. Deposits of iron ore were being mined in the hills of north-western Connecticut for several small foundries that cast iron pots. Ethan made a number of financial deals, trading, mortgaging, and borrowing until he owned the right to mine ore from a rich hill in Salisbury and to cut timber for fuel wood. He built a blast furnace to smelt the ore and eventually created the largest furnace operation in Connecticut.

Ethan was married in 1762, the same year that he opened the mine, and most historians agree that his bride was an unlikely match for the hard-drinking, well-read outdoorsman. Mary Brownson, the daughter of a successful miller, was humorless, very religious, illiterate, plain, and six years older than Ethan. After their wedding, Mary lived at the Allen family farm in Cornwall while Ethan was establishing his business in Salisbury. Their daughter Loraine was born in Cornwall, and Mary and Loraine joined Ethan in Salisbury in 1763.

The demand for potash created a demand for many iron pots, and Ethan's business flourished. He negotiated many ore, real estate, and iron deals, and he made a lot of money. He purchased additional woodlands, hired men to build roads to access new stands of timber and veins of ore, and built dams to harness the streams. He ultimately built the largest iron factory in the territory; a furnace twenty-four feet tall that employed fifty men and could produce two tons of iron at a time.

Ethan bought an excellent house on ninety-five acres. When he sold his brother Heman a half-interest in the property, Heman moved into the house with Ethan, Mary, and Loraine. Heman also bought into the iron business. Having Heman as a partner gave Ethan more time to devote to real estate deals and late-night discussions at the tavern—two of his favorite pastimes.

Most people were unaware of the dangers of alcohol in Ethan's day, and heavy drinking was more common than it is today. Even judged by the relaxed standards of his times, however, Ethan drank far too much, and alcoholism probably contributed to some of the health problems that he and other members of his family suffered.

The rowdy aspects of Ethan's personality became more noticeable once he had achieved a little leisure time. Both Ethan and Heman were fined in court several times for offenses such as disturbing the peace, blasphemy, and assault. Ethan held some radical beliefs that he didn't mind sharing in his loud voice. If anyone was foolish enough to argue with him, the huge brawler wouldn't hesitate to settle the disagreement with his fists. Before long, Ethan was at odds with the more religious and conservative citizens of the area. Growing tired of Salisbury, Ethan moved his family in the fall of 1765 to Northampton, Massachusetts, but he didn't find Northampton to his liking either. He became a partner in a lead mine there, but his outrageous behavior got him booted out of town by the selectmen in 1767. He took his family back to comparatively liberal Salisbury, where Heman, who was still living there, had converted the big house into a successful general store. Ethan, Mary, and Loraine shared the upstairs living quarters with Heman, who was still single.

Ethan was restless and needed a change. His chance came when word reached him of the New Hampshire Grants, the land of opportunity that waited beyond the frontier.

3

The New Hampshire Land Grants

GOVERNOR BENNING WENTWORTH, the first governor of New Hampshire, began to grant land charters for the wilderness area that lay between the Connecticut River and Lake Champlain in 1749. He shrewdly reserved at least two good lots for himself in each grant. He chartered the town of Bennington, named for himself, in 1750, despite claims by the colony of New York that the area rightfully belonged to it. Between 1749 and 1764, Governor Wentworth granted about three million acres of land in 138 townships, and settlers began to clear land and build homes in these townships. The area was commonly called the New Hampshire Grants by the early 1760s.

The western boundary of the colony of New Hampshire was not well defined at that time. In fact, many of the colonial boundaries were vague. This confusion was caused by the fact that the boundaries had been set by King George of England, who had never seen the colonies. In addition, maps of the American wilderness were both rare and inaccurate. But since New Hampshire had once been a part of Massachusetts, and since the western boundary of Massachusetts extended to an imaginary line twenty miles east of the Hudson River, Governor Wentworth assumed that the western boundary of New Hampshire extended to the same imaginary line. This seems like a reasonable assumption, but New York objected to it after Bennington was established, claiming that New York's territory extended east all the way to the Connecticut River.

This was not the first time that rights to the beautiful country between the Connecticut River and Lake Champlain had been disputed. The Iroquois Indians had fought with various Algonquin tribes there, and later the French and the British clashed over the same territory. Many times both Lake Champlain and the Connecticut River had been used as watery "highways" for French and Indians from Canada to raid settlements in New York, New Hampshire, and Massachusetts. The British finally claimed the area, and their control was officially established by the Treaty of Paris in 1763. After that, it was the British colonies of New York and New Hampshire that quarreled over the territory.

New York objected to Wentworth's claims and demanded that the Bennington grant be withdrawn. Governor Wentworth and Governor Cadwallader Colden of New York agreed to let King George settle the matter, and in 1764 (while Ethan Allen was busy making iron in Salisbury), the king ruled in favor of New York, giving it the right to the New Hampshire Grants. It is understandable that the king sided with the powerful landholders of New York, a colony where the people were sharply divided by social classes. The labor of the tenant farmers usually lined the pockets of the ruling class, a concept the king was familiar with in England.

On the other hand, the Grants had a nearly classless society, with very little distinction between the richest and the poorest people. The king's ruling did not settle the matter in the Grants. In fact, the disagreement was just beginning to heat up.

About two hundred families had already settled in the New Hampshire Grants, clearing the timber from the land, planting crops, and building cabins. Governor Colden decided that the king's ruling meant that Governor Wentworth had never had the authority to issue grants in the disputed area to them, so Colden attempted to regrant land that was already inhabited or at least reserved. New York surveyors came into the Grants in 1765, stretching their measuring chains across homesteads without bothering to ask permission from the settlers.

The settlers had invested years of labor and all their money in carving homes from the wilderness and were naturally angered by the prospect of seeing everything they had worked for taken away with a stroke of King George's pen. In fact, they were fighting mad and unwilling to either leave their homes or pay again for land they had already bought. To make matters worse, Governor Colden was charging two hundred to two hundred and fifty pounds per grant, compared with the twenty pounds that Governor Wentworth had charged.

The outraged Grants landowners petitioned the king to stop the surveying. The king might have settled the matter once and for all at this time if he had made a firm decision. Unfortunately, he only ordered New York in 1767 to stop issuing grants on land that had already been claimed, at least until the situation had been studied.

The dispute between New Hampshire and New York was made worse by the deep social and economic differences between the two colonies. New York was controlled by rich aristocrats who owned huge manors where poor tenant farmers did the work. New Hampshire, on the other hand, was divided into smaller farms that the owners worked themselves. This basic difference between the two colonies got in the way of a quick solution to the dispute.

The disputed territory, with its vast area of unsettled land, proved irresistible to Ethan Allen. When he needed a change, the new territory and the possibility of a fight beckoned to him.

4

◆

Disputed Claims

Many poor and restless men headed north in the 1760s in search of opportunity. When news of the Grants reached Ethan in Connecticut, he remembered that country fondly from his march during the French and Indian Wars. He had always wanted to return to the wild territory between Lake Champlain and the Connecticut River, and his interest in land investments, plus his desire to leave his conservative, religious neighbors behind, urged him toward the Grants. Ethan soon left his family in Heman's care and traveled north.

At the time when Ethan made his first solitary journey into the Grants, the area was a frontier wilderness. About four hundred people lived around Bennington and along the banks of the Connecticut River near Fort Dummer. A few lonely veterans of the French and Indian Wars lived like hermits in the big woods, and there were still a few Abenaki Indians and a couple of small French settlements in the Champlain Valley. But most of the territory was uninhabited.

Ethan roamed the wild country by himself, living off the land as he scouted the terrain. At dusk one night in the late autumn the giant woodsman got caught in a hard rain and became totally soaked. The rain then turned into snow. The temperature dropped throughout the night, leaving Ethan in serious danger of freezing to death, but he remained alive by forcing himself to walk in a circle all night in the snow. His slow trudging got more and more difficult as the night progressed, and his body stiffened in the cold. He fell down several times because his legs grew numb and wouldn't work properly. Every time he fell down, he wanted to just lie still and fall asleep, but he knew that he would never wake up if he slept, so he always struggled back onto his feet to resume his grim march around the circular path. Ethan had never been so glad to see the dawn as he was when that awful night finally ended.

All that winter Ethan snowshoed through the Grants, exploring the wilderness. He crossed over the Green Mountains and eventually worked his way to the Connecticut River, which he followed downstream to Northampton. Then he headed overland back to Salisbury. Although it was nice to be home, his extended trip had increased his interest in the Grants.

The king's lack of decisive action in the Grants dispute had left the area open for people to buy and sell land in any way they wanted. Adventurers and settlers purchased New Hampshire grants at very low prices and flocked into the area, tripling the Grants population between 1767 and 1769. New York was unhappy about this brisk trade because any money spent on a New Hampshire Grant did not end up in the New York treasury. New York responded by issuing a series of new grants on the lands claimed by New Hampshire, in direct defiance of the king's orders to stop issuing new grants.

No one knows exactly what Ethan Allen looked like because no portrait exists. Generations of artists have taken their best guesses, however, and this composite sketch from the 1800s relies on descriptions of Ethan by his contemporaries. (Photograph by George Keiser, courtesy of the Ethan Allen Homestead)

The combative atmosphere in the Grants was perfect for a man of Ethan Allen's talents. In the spring of 1770, realizing that the situation was growing more tense, Ethan attended a meeting of Salisbury residents who owned land in the Grants. He used his persuasive powers to earn selection by the landowners to go to Portsmouth, the capital of New Hampshire, to seek advice and assistance from the governor. John Wentworth, Benning Wentworth's nephew, was the governor by this time. He could not do much to clear up the land dispute, but he did give Ethan a letter of recommendation and the charters of towns in the disputed land. While he was in Portsmouth, Ethan bought three pieces of land in Poultney and Castleton, perhaps figuring that he might as well become a Grants landowner if he was going to represent them.

Ethan took Wentworth's letter of recommendation to a prominent New Haven, Connecticut, lawyer named Jared Ingersoll. Ingersoll agreed to represent the interests of the Grants people against the New York authorities. A trial was set for that June in Albany, New York. When the day of the trial arrived, the rival groups that appeared contrasted sharply in appearance; the Grants farmers wore their customary humble homespun, while the New Yorkers were all dressed up in fancy suits. The case pitted hard-working common men against rich, slick aristocrats.

The trial was actually unfair from the start. Unknown to Ethan and his friends, Judge Robert Livingston, who was presiding over the case, was a rich landowner himself and had a strong personal interest in rejecting the New Hampshire claims and upholding New York rule. New York's attorney general and lieutenant governor also held New York grants in the disputed land. An unscrupulous lawyer named James Duane, who was also a "land jobber"—an investor who purchased real estate cheaply and then sold it to settlers at a large profit—represented the New York side at the trial. Several of the Connecticut men whom Ethan represented were land jobbers, too, but many of them were actually homesteading on the disputed land.

The hopes of the Grants settlers were immediately crushed at the start of the trial when Judge Livingston ruled that all the New Hampshire grants were worthless and invalid. With this ruling, the Grants settlers didn't have a legal prayer, and the sham trial was quickly concluded to New York's satisfaction.

Ethan gloomily returned to the tavern where he was staying to gather together his gear for the journey home. He was visited there by James Duane, the New York lawyer, and John Tabor Kempe, the attorney general of New York. They tried to bribe Ethan to give up his cause by offering him land, money, and a horse, and they asked him to persuade the Grants settlers to peacefully accept the judge's ruling. Duane later claimed that Ethan accepted the bribe, although Ethan always steadfastly denied that he did.

While the New Yorkers were trying to convince Ethan to accept their side of the argument, Kempe said, "We have might on our side, and you know that might often prevails against right."

"The gods of the hills are not the gods of the valley," Ethan replied. The New York officials asked him just what he meant by that strange statement. "If you will accompany me to the hills of Bennington, the sense will be made clear," said Ethan. The Yorkers, as New York officials came to be known, wisely declined his offer. Ethan returned to the Bennington area to help prepare his allies for the conflict looming ahead.

5

♦

The Green Mountain Boys

In 1770, a group of Grants men gathered at the Catamount, a tavern in Bennington. "Catamount" is another name for the cougar, an animal that the settlers appreciated as a quiet, cunning predator. A stuffed catamount sat atop a tall signpost in front of the tavern, snarling defiantly westward—the direction of New York. Inside the tavern, Ethan told the assembled settlers about the unfortunate result of the Albany trial. The men responded by preparing for armed resistance. They formed a military association and elected Ethan Allen the leader, calling him colonel-commandant. He was a good choice because, in addition to being a great fighting man, Ethan had political skills; he knew how to inspire, lead, intimidate, and negotiate.

Ethan's five hundred acres of Grants land—good land located near where Otter Creek empties into Lake Champlain—tied his fortunes to those of the New Hampshire Grants. He was committed to the Grants cause and to the band of men whom he led. Many good men joined the rough militia that Ethan commanded, including his first cousin Remember Baker, a veteran of the French and Indian Wars, and Remember's first cousin, Seth Warner. Warner, a six-foot-two-inch settler, had already spent seven years in the Bennington area and knew the surrounding woodlands intimately. Ethan's youngest brother Ira was also involved, and so was Stephen Fay, the man who owned the Catamount Tavern.

When concerned New Yorkers informed Governor Colden that Ethan Allen had organized the "Bennington Mobb," Colden swore that he would force the riffraff back into the Green Mountains. Ethan wasn't frightened by the threat; in fact, he named his gang of about three hundred young woodsmen the Green Mountain Boys. By most military standards, the Green Mountain Boys were rowdy and unpolished. They had no cannon, their only uniform was a sprig of evergreen tucked into their hatbands, and they spent much more time drinking rum and talking at the Catamount Tavern than practicing military skills. On the other hand, they were skilled woodsmen, very familiar with their home area and determined to defend their territory.

Ethan wrote articles to the *Connecticut Courant* that described the Grants dispute as a fight between "Poor, Honest Men of the Land and Princes of Privilege." Other colonial newspapers reprinted these articles, and the royal government in London eventually heard that the Grants settlers were committed to remaining on their property. Concerned people from both sides of the dispute petitioned King George, but he once again failed to make a firm decision that might have settled the matter. Meanwhile, posters of Ethan's articles were displayed throughout the Grants, inspiring the settlers to stand firm on their land.

In July 1771, Ten Eyck, a New York sheriff from Albany, traveled into the Grants with three hundred armed men.

Sheriff Eyck led his men to the Breakenridge farm in Bennington, intending to evict James Breakenridge from his farm and claim the property under the authority of New York. But Eyck was unpleasantly surprised to discover that the farmhouse was barricaded and defended by a group of armed Green Mountain Boys. When Eyck ordered his men to advance toward the fortified house, all of the Yorkers except for about thirty promptly deserted. The sheriff then read the New York writ of ejectment out loud, but the Green Mountain Boys refused to budge. When they took aim at the remaining Yorkers, the sheriff retreated.

Ethan Allen was not at the Breakenridge farm when the Green Mountain Boys frustrated Ten Eyck. He was busy in the Rutland and Pittsford area discouraging a New York surveyor named William Cockburn. Cockburn was running lines that marked the area as Yorker land when Ethan and a group of Green Mountain Boys, who had darkened their faces with soot to make themselves look like Indians, surprised him. Ethan's disguise did not prevent Cockburn from identifying him as the leader of the gang that sent him running back to New York. Ethan's reputation as a defender of the settlers in the Grants was growing.

Dr. Sam Adams, a respected citizen of Bennington, posed a difficult problem for Ethan. Dr. Adams walked around town with a pistol in his belt, saying that the trial in Albany had given New York a legal right to the Grants area. Doctors were rare and valued in the Grants, so Ethan couldn't simply run Dr. Adams out of the area, but his open display of Yorker sympathy could not be tolerated, either. Ethan solved the dilemma by ordering that Dr. Adams be tied to a chair and hoisted into the air outside the Catamount Tavern as punishment for his bad attitude. After an hour or two of twisting in the wind, the good doctor learned his lesson.

Late in 1771, Ethan, Remember Baker, Robert Cochran, and a few other Green Mountain Boys pushed some Yorker settlers off land in Rupert that Cochran owned under New Hampshire Grants, and they burned the Yorkers' buildings there to the ground. Governor Tryon, the new governor of New York, was outraged by this, and he issued posters offering a reward for the capture of Ethan Allen, Remember Baker, Robert Cochran, Seth Warner, and a few other Green Mountain Boys. An ordinary man would have been worried to learn that the governor of New York had put a price on his head, but Ethan was merely amused, and he hung a copy of the reward poster up in the Catamount Tavern. Then Ethan drew a poster of his own, offering a reward for James Duane and John Tabor Kempe, the two Yorkers who had tried to bribe him after the Albany trial. The poster said that the reward would be payable upon delivery to the Catamount Tavern. Many copies were printed in Hartford and were spread across the region, drawing many a laugh at the Yorkers' expense.

It was not so funny when a justice of the peace from Shaftsbury named John Munro attempted to collect some of the New York bounty money by capturing Remember Baker. Early one March morning in 1772, Munro led a posse to Remember's house in Arlington. They seized the gun from the mantelpiece before Remember woke up, so he had to try to defend his home against the intruders with a big broadax. A blow from a sword cut off his thumb, injuring him so badly that he could no longer swing the ax, so he retreated to the upstairs of his cabin and escaped by clawing his way through the roof. He jumped off the roof, but plunged into a deep snowdrift, got stuck, and was captured.

Mrs. Baker and her small son were slightly injured in the scuffle, but they were left behind in their cabin while Remember was thrown into a sleigh and driven toward New York. Remember's sleigh ride was horrible—he was tied up and badly beaten, wearing just his underwear in the subzero cold, and he bled heavily from his severed thumb. After his wife watched the sleigh go out of sight, she ran to the neighbors for help. Soon a dozen Green Mountain Boys came out in pursuit of the Yorker posse, and they caught up with the kidnappers at Sancoick. The Yorkers showed no stomach for a fight, and all but two of them ran away. Munro and another man were captured and taken to the Catamount Tavern, where Dr. Jonas Fay, Stephen Fay's son, treated Remember Baker, who suffered from loss of blood and exposure but eventually recovered.

Ethan was learning that he could shape public opinion by writing letters and articles. In fact, writing was one of the most powerful tools he used to help the Grants settlers. After Remember Baker's terrible experience, Ethan wrote letters to the *Connecticut Courant* blasting the Yorkers' kidnapping plot. His colorful writing style won many people over to his side.

With the might of the British Empire behind him, Governor Tryon of New York could easily have crushed the Green Mountain Boys with a show of force, but he took no such action. Encouraged by the Green Mountain Boys' victory at the Breakenridge farm, more settlers moved into the Grants, and land prices rose quickly. Ethan made an impressive profit of four hundred percent on a parcel of land that he had owned for only a few months! He now sold all of his land in Connecticut and invested heavily in Grants land. By the spring of 1772, he was one of the largest landowners in the area, and the Allen family as a whole controlled the largest amount of land, as Ethan's brothers Heman, Heber, and Ira and their first cousin Ebenezer all bought big pieces of Grants land.

New York kept sending surveyors into the Grants to mark and claim the land under New York authority. The Green Mountain Boys had a system for dealing with these intruders. The first time they caught a Yorker surveyor in the Grants, they would send him out with a firm warning not to return; if he ignored the warning and they caught him a second time, he would be whipped with a beech switch. The Green Mountain Boys caught one stubborn surveyor named Hugh Monroe several times, and they eventually beat him so severely with a whip that he passed out and was revived three times.

The settlers did allow New York lawmen to travel through the Grants to collect debts or track down criminals. If a Yorker sheriff entered the Grants to enforce New York interests in the land dispute, however, he would have to face the Green Mountain Boys. The Grants settlers considered themselves to be law-abiding citizens; they simply considered the New York claims on their land to be worthless.

When the Yorker surveyor William Cockburn returned to the Grants in 1772, Ethan led a group of Green Mountain Boys to find him. In their travels they came upon a few Yorker settlers and sent them packing out of the territory. They finally discovered Cockburn and his surveying crew running lines again near the Onion River in Bolton. They captured the surveyors, broke their compass and chains, and seized their supplies. Cockburn had been warned before and now faced punishment, so Ethan took him to Castleton for a Green Mountain Boy "trial." News of a truce with New York arrived before the trial, however, so Cockburn was released with only another warning.

Governor Tryon had called for the truce, but unfortunately it was very brief. The negotiations that followed failed because Tryon agreed to recognize only the claims of the original settlers who had owned New Hampshire land grants before New York had begun to dispute the territory. This arrangement would have bankrupted the Allens and the other Green Mountain Boys, so it was unacceptable to them. Ethan and his friends wanted no New York authority in the Grants at all. But Governor Tryon wouldn't go along with that. The talks quickly bogged down, and the Green Mountain Boys were on the prowl once again.

6

◆

The Onion River Company

Eᴛʜᴀɴ's ʙʀᴏᴛʜᴇʀ Iʀᴀ ᴠɪsɪᴛᴇᴅ the Onion River country in 1772. We know the river today by its Indian name, Winooski, which is Abenaki for "onion." Ira was very impressed with the prime land near the river, including the area where the city of Burlington stands today, and he returned to Bennington full of plans to claim that wild country. At first Ethan was uninterested in Ira's project because the Onion River was so far from the Green Mountain Boys' headquarters in Bennington. Ira convinced his brother Heman to invest two hundred pounds in the scheme, however, and Ira himself bought fifty-two rights of land and tied up the titles on another six. But then Ira almost ran out of money and had to find additional help.

When Remember Baker agreed to get involved with Ira's Onion River scheme, Ira was able to buy supplies and hire a crew of men. Ira led Remember and the other men to the Onion River area, where they found a Yorker surveyor who was interested in the same land. They captured Benjamin Stevens, who had replaced Cockburn as the New York surveyor. They let him go, but Ira gained a reputation from the incident, and New York put a hundred-pound reward on his head.

Ethan eventually got interested in the Onion River country too. In the winter of 1772-1773, Ethan, Heman, Zimri, Ira, and Remember Baker, their cousin, founded the Onion River Company, which paid the equivalent of ten cents an acre for large tracts of the remote land. This was a huge investment—advertisements printed in the *Connecticut Courant* claimed that the Onion River Company held 45,000 acres of Onion River land, insured under New Hampshire title. Ira developed into a very sharp real estate dealer, and Ethan and Remember sold some Onion River lots to investors from Salisbury. Heman sold 1,200 acres, including several hundred to Thomas Chittenden, who would later become the first governor of Vermont.

In 1773, Ira and Remember led a crew of men to blaze a trail north from Otter Creek to the Onion River, and they found a Yorker settlement along the way. When Ethan heard about the Yorkers, he summoned the Green Mountain Boys, saying that they were "going on a big wolf hunt." Ethan and a hundred of his men destroyed the Yorker settlement—they ran the settlers off, completely burned every cabin, and smashed the large grinding stones in the gristmill into little fragments. Concerned that the Yorker landowner might return, Ethan fortified what remained of the gristmill into a defensible blockhouse.

Up on the Onion River, Ethan and Ira built a fort that also served as a store. The impressive building was thirty-two feet long by twenty feet wide, with walls eight inches thick. The second story jutted out to overhang the ground floor and was fitted with thirty-two portholes for rifle barrels. The doors were strongly constructed of a double thickness, and each window was equipped with wooden blocks that were cut to fit into the window in case of attack. The roof was specially designed to be removable, in case it became ignited by fire arrows, and the building was built over a good spring that would provide water during a siege.

Despite these warlike preparations, Ethan preferred to make his point by threatening violence rather than by actually using it. Instead of burning down the cabin of a Yorker sympathizer, he would try to persuade the settler to declare loyalty to the New Hampshire Grants merely by threatening to burn the cabin. Ethan knew that it was better to gain a possible friend than to just chase an enemy away.

By 1774, a functional road was in place from Castleton to the Onion River area, and settlers started to move north. Fifty families were homesteading on Onion River land by the spring of 1775, and the flow of pioneers drove the value of land up from ten cents per acre to five dollars or even higher. By this time, the Allen family had managed to buy about 60,000 acres that were worth around $300,000. Ethan was kept busy guarding all this real estate against the advances of the government of New York, which was growing more and more angry about the exploits of the Allen family.

Governor Tryon and the New York Assembly now passed some strict laws concerning the Grants. They declared that a gathering of three or more persons in the Grants was illegal and punishable by a year in prison, and that any New York officer could injure or even kill offenders without fear of punishment. They declared that interfering with a New York official could lead to the death penalty. They raised the reward for the capture of Ethan, Remember Baker, Seth Warner, Robert Cochran, James Breakenridge, and three other

Green Mountain Boys. And they gave Ethan and several other leaders seventy days to surrender before they would be shot on sight.

The Green Mountain Boys called public meetings in Manchester and Arlington, where they condemned New York's "Bloody Law" and insisted that no one who held any New York office was welcome in the Grants. Ethan wrote several more critical letters to the newspaper. He authored a clever pamphlet called "A Brief Narrative of the Proceedings of the Government of New York," a two-hundred-page document that warned that New York land jobbers who ignored the rights of settlers in the Grants would risk death. At the same time, the pamphlet declared that the Grants settlers were loyal to His Majesty and recognized the king as the person who should decide who really controlled the land in the Grants. The pamphlet distinguished the hard-working, ordinary people of both the Grants and New York from the rich, privileged Yorker government officials, whom Ethan portrayed as villains. Ethan and his brother Levi traveled to all the New England colonies to distribute the pamphlet, selling copies at taverns for four shillings each.

While Ethan was circulating the pamphlet in Pittsfield, he met a young attorney named John Brown, who talked about the colonies rebelling against the rule of England. Brown was traveling to Canada to see if the Canadian people would be interested in cutting their ties with England. Despite his pamphlet's declaration of loyalty to the king, Ethan was excited by Brown's message. The two of them discussed how important Fort Ticonderoga, the old fort overlooking Lake Champlain, would become if rebellion against England ever became a reality. Ethan saw to it that Brown had a pair of Green Mountain Boys to serve as guides on his Canadian journey. Ethan and Brown parted with good feelings toward

each other, unaware that fate would soon bring them together again.

The bitter feelings over the land dispute continued to
grow stronger. The Green Mountain Boys captured Reverend
Benjamin Hough, an enthusiastic Yorker and Anabaptist
preacher who lived in Durham, and they conducted a farce
trial in which Ethan was the chief justice. The "court" found
Hough guilty of holding a job as a New York magistrate and
sentenced him to the harshest penalty that the Green Mountain Boys ever inflicted. Reverend Hough was bound to a
tree, where four strong men took turns beating his back with
cord whips, laying on two hundred lashes. Hough had to be
treated by a doctor before he could be led back to New York.

The Green Mountain Boys now held a meeting where
they discussed the need to prepare for an armed fight with
New York. They decided that each man must be armed with
a good flintlock rifle, a pound of black gunpowder, a supply
of lead shot, and a tomahawk. The Green Mountain Boys realized that hard times were approaching, and they vowed to
be ready.

7

◆

Trouble at Westminster Court

ALL OF THE AMERICAN COLONIES were in a state of turmoil in 1775. Revolution against the English government of King George III was openly discussed as colonists held tea riots and rebelled against the unfairly high price of sugar. In the New Hampshire Grants, liberty was an even more attractive prospect to most people than avoiding taxation without representation. Many of the settlers in the Grants were in favor of breaking away from English rule because that would transfer the authority over their land from a distant king to fellow Americans, who they hoped would understand and sympathize with their situation. There was a great deal of anger and uncertainty in all the colonies at this time, and Americans attempted to address their problems by convening the Continental Congress on March 14, 1775, in Philadelphia.

During the previous growing season, farmers had been hurt by a poor harvest, and many people in the New Hampshire Grants were almost broke. A settler who couldn't pay

off his debts faced terrible consequ
were still under New York jurisdi
outside of the Bennington area. A
owed money) could apply to the
person who owed the money)
necticut River Valley settlers
lose their farms, and they app
as Chandler, who was scheduled to ho
minster that March. Judge Chandler assured the settle
he would hear only criminal cases at that session and would
delay the debtors' hearings. This gave the farmers some extra time to settle their debts.

William Paterson, a sheriff who lived near Westminster,
received most of his money from property seizures ordered
by the court. People in the area knew that Sheriff Paterson
would want the debtors' hearings to proceed, and many of
them didn't trust Judge Chandler to postpone them indefi-
nitely. A group of local farmers decided to prevent any hearings from taking place, and they took possession of the
courthouse.

When news of the courthouse takeover reached Sheriff
Paterson, he formed a posse of twenty-five men armed with
guns. He led them into Westminster on March 13, 1775, and
approached the courthouse. The sheriff hollered to the men
inside, ordering them to clear the premises within fifteen
minutes. But the settlers jeered at the sheriff, clearly intending to ignore his order. Sheriff Paterson then led his posse to
a nearby tavern to discuss the situation and to bolster their
courage with rum punch.

Judge Chandler heard about what was happening at the
courthouse and went there to try to defuse the situation. He
told the farmers inside the courthouse that Sheriff Paterson
had been wrong to bring a gang of armed men there. The

...e men that they were welcome to remain in the
... that night, and he promised to go reason with the
...He was very persuasive, and the settlers were reas-
... Most of them left the courthouse, although a small
...up remained on sentry duty in the building.

Judge Chandler went to the tavern and talked to Sheriff Paterson for a while. After he left, the posse continued to drink. After four hours of drinking, rum overpowered the voice of reason, and at midnight Paterson led his drunken gang to the courthouse. The few settlers remaining inside the courthouse were armed only with clubs, not guns. When Sheriff Paterson tried to enter the courthouse, they pushed him back outside. He tried to force his way inside a second time, but was clubbed and thrust back.

"Fire!" the enraged sheriff yelled. The posse obeyed; their barrage of gunfire passed through the courthouse door and hit twelve settlers. A young man from Brattleboro named William French fell dead at the age of twenty-two with four bullets in his body and a fifth in his head. A man named Daniel Houghton was hurt so badly that he died nine days later. Ten other men were wounded. One deadly round of gunfire was all it took to defeat the small group of settlers. Sheriff Paterson seized the courthouse within five minutes, throwing those who could not escape in jail.

Shocked settlers sent messengers riding in every direction that night, spreading the story about the murder of decent young men by followers of King George. The people of the Grants responded quickly, and by the following night hundreds of Green Mountain Boys had gathered in Westminster. The angry mob freed the settlers who had been jailed and went on to capture Sheriff Paterson, some court officials, and all the posse members they could find. The Green Mountain Boys sent their prisoners to stand trial for murder in Northampton, Massachusetts. But the trial never took place: New York officials demanded the release of the prisoners, and the Massachusetts judges complied.

The release of Paterson and his posse outraged the citizens of Westminster, and New York court was never again convened in the Grants. The Westminster settlers held a convention in April and voted to reject New York laws. This vote induced the settlers on the eastern side of the Green Mountains to join forces with the Green Mountain Boys from around Bennington in their resistance against New York, greatly strengthening the position of Ethan Allen and his friends. Ethan was one of three men who were elected to lead the resistance against the powerful New York authorities on behalf of the people of the Grants. Ethan's excitement over this appointment was short-lived, however, because it was quickly followed by much more important news—gunshots had been fired in Lexington, Massachusetts, where American colonists had battled troops of the King of England. The American Revolution had begun.

8

◆

Fort Ticonderoga

IT WAS ELEVEN O'CLOCK AT NIGHT when Ethan Allen crammed eighty-three of his men into two boats that the Green Mountain Boys had seized on Lake Champlain. A brisk breeze whipped up large waves on the water that night, but the small rowboat and the bateau (a large, stable boat designed for the open lake), landed safely on the western shore. Then Ethan sent the boats back for the rest of the men, but he realized that the remainder of his force would not get across the lake before dawn.

Knowing that surprise was needed if his mission were to succeed, Ethan decided to attack with the small group of men who had already crossed the lake. He gathered his troops and delivered an inspiring speech, then led them to Fort Ticonderoga. They crept around the east wall and found a hole in the south wall that a spy had described in his report.

Ethan drew his sword and led the way inside, catching a lone British sentry asleep. Ethan ran at the sentry, who woke up and aimed his musket at his attacker, but when the Redcoat pulled the trigger, his weapon misfired. The sentry turned and ran, yelling an unsuccessful warning to the sleeping British troops.

Fort Ticonderoga was located on the western shore of Lake Champlain, on the southern part of the lake where the water is narrow enough that the fort's artillery could cover it. Since there were no roads there, any army that wanted to travel through the area had to move along Lake Champlain, which Fort Ticonderoga ruled. There were perhaps as many

Fort Ticonderoga sits on the New York shore of southern Lake Champlain. As can be seen in the photo above, the lake is very narrow in this area, and whoever controlled the fort could also control travel up and down the lake. (Photograph courtesy of Fort Ticonderoga)

as two hundred artillery pieces at the fort at this time, and trained British troops guarded the fort. Trying to seize such a stronghold with a group of rough frontiersmen was a very daring move.

News of Lexington and Concord spread quickly throughout the New Hampshire Grants. When Ethan Allen heard about the combat, he realized that the conflict might well be decided by whoever controlled the important military routes of the Champlain Valley. The Green Mountain Boys had become a strong fighting force in their conflict with the Yorkers, and Ethan boldly decided to lead them in an attempt to capture Fort Ticonderoga. The fort at that time was badly in need of repairs, with a breached wall, and out of all the artillery, only about two dozen cannon were actually in working order. It was manned by only about fifty British regulars, although the fort was large enough to hold hundreds of men.

About two hundred Green Mountain Boys gathered in Castleton to plan the attack on Fort Ticonderoga. They were joined by a few troops from Massachusetts and Connecticut on Sunday, May 7, 1775. Ethan Allen was unanimously elected commander of the expedition.

Ethan sent men to guard the trails leading to the fort, to make sure that no news of his mission reached the British troops. He also sent a spy, Noah Phelps, to investigate the fort's defenses. Phelps got inside the fort by pretending to be a woodcutter looking for a barber, and the report that he brought back to Ethan was encouraging. There were only fifty or sixty Redcoats in the fort, and they seemed to be careless—they hadn't even heard about the battles at Lexington and Concord, and they maintained poor security at Ticonderoga. In fact, a small section of the south wall had fallen down sometime before, creating an opening through the defenses.

Ethan and his group of 230 men assembled in Shoreham, barely two miles across the lake from Fort Ticonderoga, on the night of May 9, 1775. They were waiting for boats to ferry them to the western shore when Colonel Benedict Arnold arrived.

At the start of the American Revolution, Benedict Arnold had been a successful druggist and bookseller worth more than $12,000, which was a lot of money in those days. When he heard about the battles at Lexington and Concord on April 20, 1775, he left his secure life behind the very next day. On April 30, Arnold appeared before the Massachusetts Committee of Safety and proposed to lead an expedition to capture Fort Ticonderoga and a smaller fort at Crown Point. He received a commission as a colonel in the Continental Army, and his orders were to recruit four hundred men and take Fort Ticonderoga. He was issued ammunition, a hundred pounds in cash, and a couple of horses.

When Benedict Arnold caught up with the Green Mountain Boys at Shoreham, he had only one man with him, his servant. Arnold tried to take command of the force, but the expedition members had elected Ethan Allen their leader. They weren't impressed by the chubby Arnold in his shiny, brand-new uniform. A brief argument produced a compromise: Arnold was allowed to march along with Ethan, but he had no authority over the troops.

After Ethan's close call with the sentry, the Green Mountain Boys raced onto the parade ground inside the fort, cheering and whooping. They ran to the barracks and battered through the doors of the sleeping quarters, capturing many of the surprised British before they could organize an effective defense.

The sentry whose gun had misfired charged the intruders with his bayonet. He came close to wounding one of the

Green Mountain Boys—some historians think he did wound one man—but Ethan quickly stopped the attack by whacking the sentry on the head with the flat of his sword. The dazed sentry dropped his musket. Ethan grabbed him and demanded to know where the commanding officer was. The shaking sentry pointed to a barracks staircase. Ethan leaped up the stairs, followed by a panting Benedict Arnold.

According to popular legend, Ethan was met at the top of the staircase by Captain William Delaplace, the British commander of Fort Ticonderoga, who was drowsy and carried his breeches in his hands. When Ethan demanded the immediate surrender of the fort, Captain Delaplace had enough composure to ask by whose authority. Ethan paused a moment before making his famous reply: "In the name of the great Jehovah and the Continental Congress." Not all historians accept this tale, however. Some insist that this impressive response was composed at a later date, and that what Ethan actually said was, "Come out of there, you damned rat!" It is also uncertain whether it was indeed Captain Delaplace or really Lieutenant Feltham, a younger British officer, who was caught "with his pants down." The famous story of the unprepared captain being surprised by the daring frontiersman is appealing, however, and it has lasted for more than two hundred years.

Despite the disagreement over the exact sequence of events, there is no doubt that Captain Delaplace was soon persuaded to surrender his command. The British troops were ordered to be paraded without arms, and Ethan Allen and the Green Mountain Boys took possession of the fort. They had accomplished a major military coup without loss of life on either side, or even a single shot fired. The wounded British sentry was bandaged and provided with enough rum to ease his pain.

The victorious frontiersmen took nearly sixty adult male prisoners, plus forty women and children, and treated all of them decently. The expedition also captured many valuable artillery pieces for the war. Again, accounts vary as to how many pieces they captured; one report states that they captured more than a hundred cannon, a thirteen-inch mortar, several howitzers, and many swivel guns. Another estimates that they seized fourteen mortars, two howitzers, forty-three cannon with bores up to five and a half inches, gunpowder, ten tons of musket and cannon balls, and three cartloads of flints. Benedict Arnold claimed that they captured about two hundred artillery pieces in all. Whatever the exact number, the artillery they captured played an important part in the war. The Continental Congress wanted the Ticonderoga artillery to be stored at Lake George until it could be returned to the king after harmony was restored, but Ethan refused to go along with such a stupid plan. The following December, General George Washington ordered the cannon removed. The cannon reached him on January 24, and he promptly used it to blow the British out of Boston.

The conquest of Ticonderoga also yielded a supply of food, several boats, and a generous amount of rum. After securing the prisoners, Ethan gave Captain Delaplace a receipt for ninety gallons of rum, and the Green Mountain Boys started to celebrate. They passed a bowl full of the liquor from hand to hand, as was the custom in those days, toasting liberty, the Continental Congress, the freedom of America, and the gray morning of May 10, 1775.

Benedict Arnold was disgusted by the drinking, which he considered unmilitary. He also disliked the shabby clothes of the woodsmen and their lack of military discipline. He later complained about Ethan Allen and his rebels, claiming that he had been "often insulted by him and his officers, often threatened with my life, and twice shot at by his men." There certainly was not much affection between the Green Mountain Boys and the fancy gentleman who had hoped to command them.

It was still early morning when Seth Warner and the rear guard finally crossed the lake to Fort Ticonderoga. Seth was disappointed that he had missed the action, so Ethan sent him north with a hundred men to capture the smaller fortification at Crown Point. Seth and his group succeeded on the same day, capturing the British sergeant and twelve soldiers who were guarding Crown Point. They also seized more artillery pieces.

This classic scene of Ethan Allen demanding the surrender of Fort Ticonderoga was painted in the early twentieth century by an unknown artist. Nathan Beman is the young man holding the lantern. (Courtesy of Fort Ticonderoga)

The capture of Fort Ticonderoga without the loss of a single human life established Ethan Allen as a hero of the Revolution. It was the first offensive military action by the rebels and the first victory. Lexington and Concord had both been defensive actions, and neither could be considered a victory for the Americans. Ticonderoga was the most famous fort in the colonies, filled with valuable artillery, and the Green Mountain Boys' victory sent a message of hope to the rebel cause. The image of Ethan Allen's large figure standing with drawn sword while demanding the surrender of the fort from a trembling British officer with his breeches in his hands became a colorful symbol of the Revolution.

9

♦

Planning an Invasion of Canada

THE GREEN MOUNTAIN BOYS drank up the supply of rum at Fort Ticonderoga within four days. They were still recovering from their celebrations on May 14, when one hundred troops arrived to fight under Benedict Arnold. Arnold wasted no time putting his new recruits to work. The Green Mountain Boys had previously captured a schooner, and Arnold sailed it with fifty of the men to capture the British garrison at St. John's on May 18. Arnold also captured the thirteen British soldiers who were stationed at St. John's, plus five bateaux and an armed sloop, which was the only real warship on the lake at that time. He accomplished the victory without losing a single man.

Ethan had hoped to take part in the attack on St. John's, but the swift schooner had left him and his four bateaux full of Green Mountain Boys behind. After his victory, Arnold abandoned St. John's and headed back toward Ticonderoga, meeting the bateaux full of Green Mountain Boys on the way.

This blunderbuss was made in London, England in 1714 by T. Green. It is thought that Ethan Allen gave it to Benedict Arnold on May 10, 1775, the morning the Green Mountain Boys captured Fort Ticonderoga. Arnold in turn gave it to Jonathan Trumbull. Note the words "Ethan Allen" carved in the stock. (Photograph courtesy of Fort Ticonderoga)

Arnold invited Ethan aboard for a toast of rum. (Arnold had no objections to the drinking now that he was triumphant.) While he was aboard the schooner, Ethan told Arnold that he planned to proceed to St. John's and use it as a base of operations for an attack on Canada. Arnold advised against this plan, since he considered St. John's to be difficult to defend, but Ethan went ahead with his scheme anyway.

Ethan's mission at St. John's was placed in jeopardy when Governor Guy Carleton sent two hundred of his eight hundred British regulars from Montreal toward St. John's. A scout informed Ethan about the presence of the British troops when they were at the Sorel River. Ethan's first inclination was to ambush the British, but some of his more cautious men talked him out of it. Instead, he led the Green Mountain Boys across the river to the east bank, away from the British, to await developments. Ethan's men were caught by

surprise when the British crossed the river at dawn with cannon, and the Green Mountain Boys fled the area, leaving
three men behind in their haste. Two of the abandoned men
were able to walk home, but one was captured, and Ethan's
reputation was hurt by the incident.

When spring arrived in the Grants country, the Green
Mountain Boys were needed at home to plant their crops.
They began to leave Fort Ticonderoga to plow and sow their
fields, eventually leaving Ethan with very few men. Meanwhile, more paid troops were arriving from the east to serve
under Benedict Arnold, which swung the balance of power
away from Ethan. Ethan conceded the point and handed over
the command to Arnold on May 27.

Ethan was still enthusiastic about his idea to attack Canada before the British were prepared in the north. He had ex-
perienced the value of a surprise attack at Ticonderoga, and
he was confident that he could succeed in Canada as well.
He wrote to several Canadian residents and Indian tribes,
looking for possible allies for his assault. Thinking that he
might be able to use Ile-aux-Noix, near St. John's, as a military base, he sent Remember Baker on a scouting mission to
determine whether the island would be easy to defend.

While Remember Baker and the men he led were inves-
tigating the island, they left their boat unguarded on the
shore. A passing band of Caughnawaga Indians happened to
discover it and took it. Remember spotted them paddling
past the island, and he threatened to shoot them from his
high vantage point if they didn't return his boat. The Indians kept going and Remember took aim, but his gun misfired, and then an Indian shot him dead. A little while later,
a larger force of Indians returned to the scene and chased the
Green Mountain Boys off the island. Then the Indians cut off
Remember's head and took it to St. John's, triumphantly dis-

playing their grisly trophy on the end of a pole. The British at St. John's were not amused by this conduct, and they re-united Remember's head and body in a Christian burial. Ethan was devastated by the news of his cousin's death, and the Caughnawaga Indians and the Green Mountain Boys were bitter enemies from that day on.

The Grants settlers formed a Committee of War, which in June 1775 sent Ethan Allen and Seth Warner to Philadelphia to address the Continental Congress. Ethan and Seth proposed an invasion of Canada and the reinstatement of Ethan as commander of Fort Ticonderoga. Some of the members of Congress were not fond of the Green Mountain Boys because of their dispute with New York, but old disagreements were ignored for the moment as everyone knew that they had to work together to defeat the British. Congress approved the invasion of Canada, provided that the American General Philip Schuyler agreed with the idea.

Ethan and Seth left Philadelphia and traveled to New York City to address the New York Assembly. Congress had recommended that New York hire the Green Mountain Boys to help fight the British, and Seth and Ethan delivered the recommendation in person. This required quite a bit of courage on their part since the New York Assembly had recently recommended that the two Green Mountain Boy leaders be shot on sight. Times had changed, however, and now the Yorkers desperately needed skilled fighters to battle the British. Everyone knew that the Green Mountain Boys were brave, strong, and stealthy, so the New York Assembly set aside their bitterness and commissioned the formation of a militia force of five hundred Green Mountain Boys, with back pay due from the date of Fort Ticonderoga's capture.

In late July, Ethan returned to Fort Ticonderoga, where he learned that General Schuyler had assumed command from

Benedict Arnold. Ethan remained at Ticonderoga, but perhaps he should have traveled to Dorset for a July 26 meeting. There, committees from several Grants towns met to elect the officers of the new militia. They elected Seth Warner as commander, Heman Allen and Heber Allen as captains, and Ira Allen as lieutenant. But Ethan Allen, the hero of Ticonderoga who had risked his life to stand before the New York Assembly and argue for the formation of the militia, was completely overlooked!

If the Green Mountain Boys had been doing the voting in Dorset, there is little doubt that Ethan would have been elected commander, but a large turnout of people who disapproved of Ethan's rowdiness and drinking swayed the elections. Many men who had been deeply offended by Ethan in the past were now able to gain some revenge at the polls. Yorker sympathizers and elderly, religious, and/or self-righteous citizens who considered Ethan a wild, brawling, hard-drinking heretic (an image that Ethan no doubt proudly agreed with) all voted for a change in leadership.

A lesser man might have sulked after being so ignored, but Ethan shrugged the officers' election off. He realized that his fighting men still had faith in him even if the old farmers did not, and he approached General Schuyler to offer his services in any position. Ethan wasn't asking for a commission or rank—he simply wanted to aid the Revolution in whatever way he could. Schuyler was reluctant to have anything to do with him at first, despite the fact that Ethan was a proven leader, but Seth Warner and many of the Green Mountain Boys urged Schuyler to reconsider. In fact, many of the woodsmen absolutely refused to serve under anyone except Ethan Allen. Schuyler soon realized that he was going to have to employ Ethan somewhere. In the end, he granted him a position as a civilian scout of the northern territories, provided that Ethan did not meddle in military affairs.

Ethan was happy to accept his position as civilian scout. He was still convinced that the Americans should attack Canada quickly before the British had a chance to organize their defenses, and he repeatedly advised this course of action to Schuyler. The general had not held Ethan's advice in very high esteem since the Dorset election, however, and he lingered at Fort Ticonderoga while the British strengthened their position in the north.

General Schuyler suffered from gout, a disease that causes the joints to swell painfully, and it finally got so bad that it sent him packing to Saratoga. General Richard Montgomery then assumed command of Fort Ticonderoga, which was good news for Ethan because Montgomery had a good opinion of him. In late August 1775, Montgomery received intelligence that the British were building several ships at St. John's. This was a serious development, because a few enemy ships could threaten Benedict Arnold's armed sloop. General Montgomery decided that the British shipbuilding merited investigation. With fifty bateaux and 1,200 men at his disposal, he sent an expedition to St. John's on August 28, 1775.

Ethan was still serving as a civilian scout, but with his tremendous self-confidence he was convinced that he had every right to take command if he felt he was needed. Montgomery probably didn't feel the same way, although he certainly held the Allen family in high esteem; Ira was a trusted scout and messenger at Montgomery's headquarters. Ethan really wanted to lead a force to attack St. John's (and maybe regain some of the respect that he had lost on his earlier trip there), but General Montgomery declined his request. He chose instead to assign Ethan to a task for which he was well suited: persuading Canadians to aid the American cause.

Ethan carried letters into Canada that assured the French Canadians that the Americans would not prohibit their Catholic religion if they defeated the British. Ethan hoped to gather information about British military strength while he was in the region, but his main goal was to convince the French and the Canadian Indians that the Americans had no quarrel with either of them and wanted to fight only the British. Ethan traveled far into Canada with a group of concerned Canadians and a few Green Mountain Boys, and he successfully roused the people, recruiting 250 armed Canadians within a four-day period.

After a week of fanning the flames of revolution in Canada, Ethan encountered another group of men who were performing a similar task, led by Major John Brown—the same John Brown whom Ethan had met while distributing his pamphlets in Massachusetts. Major Brown and Ethan had an interesting reunion, and Brown suggested an idea that was irresistible to Ethan but that proved to be disastrous: Major Brown proposed an attack on Montreal.

10

◆

Attack on Montreal

Ethan EAGERLY AGREED to Major Brown's idea for a surprise attack on Montreal because it was precisely the sort of daring maneuver that appealed to him. Ethan himself had been advocating a quick strike in Canada for quite some time, and he was delighted to find someone else with the same bold personality. Major Brown had about two hundred fighting men with him at that time, and although Ethan had been sending his recruits to Fort Ticonderoga, he had about 110 men traveling with him, so they decided to launch a two-pronged attack.

Major Brown's plan called for Ethan to locate enough canoes to ferry his men across the St. Lawrence River north of Montreal, while Brown and his troops crossed the river to the south of Montreal. The two forces would then attack simultaneously from opposite directions. Ethan agreed to the plan, but a few complications developed. His party was able to locate only enough canoes to carry one-third of the men at a time, so it took three trips to complete the crossing. The river was also extremely rough—a strong wind whipped up white-caps on the water. But Ethan managed to assemble his men north of Montreal before dawn.

As a signal to attack, Major Brown was supposed to lead his men in three cheers at dawn, but when dawn came and went with no signal, Ethan knew that Brown had let him down. Perhaps the major had considered the wild St. Lawrence too dangerous to cross that night, or maybe he couldn't find any canoes. Whatever the reason, Ethan never printed a harsh word about Brown, and you can be certain that Ethan would have voiced his anger if he had blamed Brown.

Major Brown's failure to appear left Ethan in a terrible situation. Since only one-third of his men could ride in the canoes at a time, he couldn't retreat across the river without abandoning most of his men to the British, who would be sure to notice the retreat during daylight. Ethan did the best he could under the circumstances, selecting a defensible location and placing sentries on the road in each direction. Then he dispatched two messengers asking for help, one to Major Brown and another to a Mr. Walker, a sympathetic Canadian who lived nearby. Ethan's guards detained everyone who came along the road because they wanted to keep their presence a secret from the British for as long as possible. Unfortunately, one of their prisoners escaped and went to L'Assomption, where Mr. Walker had formed a substantial squad to come to Ethan's aid. When Mr. Walker learned from the escaped prisoner that Ethan's position was very vulnerable, he thought better of joining the coming battle and sent his men home, leaving Ethan and his small force to their own defenses.

When Governor Guy Carleton first heard that there was a band of rebels nearby, he immediately got ready to flee

Montreal in his armed schooner, the *Gaspée*. Before the ship set sail, however, Carleton received a report describing the small size of the Yankee force. This restored the governor's courage, and he decided to attack the intruders. He assembled a force that included only forty British regulars but nearly four hundred Canadians and Indians.

Scouts delivered to Ethan the bad news that Carleton was preparing to attack with a force four times as large as Ethan's. Ethan calmly got ready and persuaded his men to hold their ground. He positioned them behind the best available cover and among a few scattered buildings, taking advantage of logs, ditches, and posts for shelter. When Carleton attacked at two o'clock in the afternoon, Ethan sent a Canadian named Richard Young to the bank of the St. Lawrence with nine men to protect his left flank, and he ordered the rest of his troops to shoot from behind their cover. Carleton launched a frontal assault first, then detached a number of men to flank Ethan on the right. Ethan ordered Canadian volunteer John Dugan and fifty of the Canadian recruits to move to the right to meet the flanking attack. This would have been a good strategic move except that Dugan and all his men deserted. Young and his men on the left flank ran away, too, and the deserters took the canoes. Ethan was left with only forty-five men, some of them wounded, and they were nearly surrounded by the enemy.

Ethan bravely led his men on a desperate retreat, fighting on the run for over a mile before his enemies closed in and brought him to a halt. Ethan stood his ground as a British officer ran up and shot at him, but the officer was panting so hard from the chase that he missed. Ethan then took a shot back at the officer, but he missed too. Ethan yelled to the British officer, offering to surrender if he and his men would be treated as honorable prisoners of war rather than

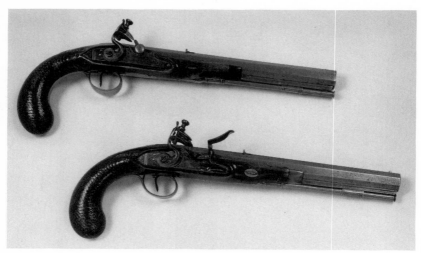

These dueling pistols were made in England in the late 1700s. They are said to have been owned by Ethan Allen, but it is very difficult to prove whether or not he did in fact own them. They are currently part of the Fort Ticonderoga Museum collection. (Photograph courtesy of Fort Ticonderoga)

as traitors. The officer agreed to the terms, accepting Ethan's sword and the surrender of thirty-eight men, including seven who were wounded.

No sooner had Ethan handed over his sword than an Indian brave ran at Ethan, yelling loud war whoops. Realizing that the Indian had no intention of honoring the terms of his surrender, Ethan grabbed the British officer and used the man as a human shield. Keeping the officer in front of him, he spun to avoid the Indian's attempts to shoot him. Then a second brave joined in the attempt to kill Ethan, and they might have succeeded if an Irish soldier hadn't come to Ethan's defense. The Irishman used his bayonet to convince the Indians to back away from Ethan and the British officer.

In the field, Ethan's British captors treated him with respect, but he received a different reception back at the garrison. When British General Richard Prescott realized that he was facing the infamous Ethan Allen, capturer of Fort Ticonderoga, the pompous general became furious. He angrily ordered his sergeant to execute as traitors the Canadian men who had fought for the rebels. Ethan was shocked by this order, which ignored the conditions of his surrender. He ripped open his shirt and presented his naked chest to the general, asking that he himself be bayoneted before the men who had served under him were harmed. This gesture worked; the Canadian lives were spared. Prescott didn't kill anyone on the spot, but he did threaten Ethan with hanging: "I will not execute you now, but you shall grace a halter at Tyburn."

11

◆

Ethan the Prisoner

GENERAL PRESCOTT CONSIDERED ETHAN ALLEN to be a traitor and a villain, and he did what he could to ensure that the proud conqueror of Fort Ticonderoga was treated harshly. Ethan was confined on the *Gaspée* in handcuffs, and his ankles were chained to irons that weighed about thirty-five pounds and that were secured to an eight-foot bar. A hard wooden trunk was the only furniture in the dark hold of his prison, serving as both chair and bed. The iron bar kept him firmly anchored and prevented him from lying down in any position except flat on his back with his knees bent and his feet held down near the bar.

The British officer in charge of the *Gaspée*, Captain Royal, was upset by the shameful treatment of his prisoner. Captain Royal was unable to reduce Ethan's suffering, however, because General Prescott was stubborn and refused to grant Ethan's request to loosen his bonds enough to allow him to change position. A sentry with a bayonet attached to his rifle was stationed to guard Ethan around the clock, despite the fact that a sentry was unnecessary for security reasons. Ethan was never granted a moment alone even when he needed to relieve himself.

Some of the British treated Ethan with more compassion than General Prescott. A Lieutenant Bradley arranged for Ethan to receive good food from the officers' mess and a ration of grog (watered-down rum) every day. One of the enlisted men assigned to guard Ethan brought in two small blocks of wood to raise the iron bar just enough to prevent it from thrusting against Ethan's sore ankles when he lay on his back to sleep. These simple favors eased Ethan's discomfort considerably. One of his helpers provided Ethan with writing materials, and he wrote several letters to General Prescott and at least one to Governor Carleton, reminding them of the decent treatment that his British prisoners had received at Ticonderoga and asking for an improvement in his own situation. Ethan never received an answer to his appeals, however, and he suffered on the *Gaspée* for six long weeks.

Finally Ethan was transferred downstream in the charge of a Captain McCloud, who treated him decently and took off the heavy leg irons. At the end of a tolerable journey, Ethan was delivered to a vessel anchored off Quebec. Captain Littlejohn, the commander of this ship, treated Ethan honorably, allowing him the run of the ship unfettered by chains and housing him in the officer's quarters during the nine or ten days that Ethan was aboard. Then in November Ethan was moved to yet another ship, the dispatch carrier *Adamant*, which was under the command of a spiteful man named Brook Watson, who made certain that his prisoners suffered terribly.

All of the surviving men who had been captured with Ethan at Montreal were loaded aboard the *Adamant*; thirty-four prisoners were packed belowdecks into a dim, stuffy area measuring twenty by twenty-two feet. They were allowed no water to wash with, and the only furnishings in the cramped quarters were two tubs for the prisoners' bodily wastes. The crew of the *Adamant* amused themselves by harassing the captives. They spat on Ethan and his men and taunted them with the prospect of hanging. As horrible as the conditions were at first, they became worse during the long voyage as the prisoners became increasingly dirty, infested with lice, and sick with fever and diarrhea. The smell of the overcrowded, filthy hold became unbearable as the unwashed men and their tubs of waste grew increasingly rank. Ethan was convinced that the British were intentionally feeding them a diet of mostly salt meat and then allowing them barely enough water to survive in order to make them suffer from thirst. It was the small amount of rum issued to them each day that kept the prisoners alive, he thought.

Somehow all the prisoners survived the terrible voyage and arrived alive on December 22, 1775, at Falmouth, in Cornwall, England. The prisoners were paraded through the streets toward Pendennis Castle. The roads were crowded with a mob that the British soldiers had to beat back with their swords in order to move forward. Ethan presented an impressive figure despite the hardships of his journey, and the English people were fascinated by the enormous frontiersman, whose attire must have seemed outlandish to them. Ethan wore homespun breeches, heavy nailed shoes, worsted stockings, a deerskin jacket, and a vivid red woolen cap, all badly in need of washing. His hair and beard had grown long because the prisoners hadn't been allowed the luxury of a barber.

The first thing that Ethan did upon arriving at Pendennis Castle was to write a letter to the Continental Congress. He must have been aware that the letter would never be delivered, and quite likely he knew perfectly well who would actually read it. The letter described in detail the terrible treatment that he and his men had suffered, and it cleverly recommended that Congress not take revenge on any British prisoners until it could be seen if conditions for Ethan and his men improved in England. What Ethan didn't know was that by the time he wrote his letter, the Americans had taken several hundred British soldiers prisoner, which strengthened his position considerably. Ethan would have been delighted to learn that the same General Prescott who had treated him so badly was now a prisoner himself, slapped in irons and threatened with severe punishment for his ill treatment of Ethan. Prime Minister Lord North read Ethan's letter, and after the Cabinet considered its merits, conditions for the prisoners at Pendennis Castle improved.

Ethan started receiving good meals regularly, accompanied by wine delivered daily from the commandant's provisions. He was marched around the castle yard to entertain some of the fancy ladies and gentlemen, who had never met anyone like the huge, colorful woodsman. Ethan appreciated the chance to walk outdoors again, and he truly enjoyed the opportunity to speak in public. On several occasions, he was able to address the noble folk in a castle garden, and as usual, his native wit served him well.

One time a group of very religious people asked Ethan if he was ready to meet his fate in the afterlife, should he be hanged. Ethan replied that he knew little about the spirit world but anticipated being "as well treated as other gentlemen of my merit." Spirited remarks like that earned Ethan the respect of many of his distinguished visitors as they discussed politics, philosophy, religion, and other interesting subjects with him. Ethan took the opportunity to plead for the revolutionary cause, insisting that the colonies must be granted freedom from an overbearing government that was far removed, both geographically and philosophically, from America.

One day a generous nobleman called for some rum punch for the prisoner, and a servant brought some in. Ethan declined to receive the punch bowl from the hands of a servant, insisting that the nobleman hand him the bowl himself, as an equal. His visitor graciously accommodated him and handed Ethan the large punch bowl, which the frontiersman chugged down all at once, astounding his British acquaintances with his drinking ability.

During the two weeks when Ethan was attracting attention at the castle, his fate and that of his fellow prisoners was being hotly argued in Parliament and in the newspapers. Ethan's performances with the aristocrats made good copy and fueled the fires of debate. A lot of people believed that the rebels deserved to hang, and when the captives were moved from the castle to the frigate *Solebay,* the ship's crew produced a hangman's noose and waved it at the prisoners. Ethan believed that they were about to be executed, but the sailors were only having a little cruel fun. Instead of being hanged as common criminals, Ethan and several other captives were transported back to America as prisoners of war.

Captain Symonds, the commander of the *Solebay,* strictly forbade the prisoners to appear on deck. He singled out Ethan in particular and pointed out that walking on deck was reserved for gentlemen. At first Ethan obeyed the order because he was worried that the British were planning to dispose of their annoying captives by murdering them and dumping their bodies into the ocean. But his fears soon subsided and after two days he bathed and shaved and put in an appearance on deck. Captain Symonds angrily reminded

Ethan that he had been ordered to stay off the deck. Ethan replied: "And at the same time you said it is the place for gentlemen to walk. I am Colonel Allen. I don't believe we have been properly introduced." After that Ethan was allowed to stroll about the deck, as long as he avoided walking on the same side of the ship as the irritable Captain Symonds, who every now and then would order Ethan to go down into the hold. Whenever that happened, Ethan would simply wait for Symonds to leave the deck and then come topside once again.

An Irish petty officer named Gilligan took a liking to Ethan and offered to share his quarters with him. Gilligan's stateroom was extremely small, but it was definitely an improvement over the prisoners' hold. Ethan gratefully accepted the offer and roomed with Gilligan all the way to America.

Sailing as part of a British fleet, the *Solebay* encountered a severe storm near Cork, Ireland. After the *Solebay* survived the tempest, it dropped anchor at Cork, and Captain Symonds went ashore. While he was gone, a group of generous Irish merchants visited the American prisoners and gave each of them a suit of clothes with two shirts, an overcoat, six pounds of sugar, and two pounds of tea. Ethan received eight good shirts, silk hose, a number of pairs of woolen hose, two pairs of shoes, a beaver hat, another beaver hat trimmed with gold lace, enough broadcloth to produce two fine suits, fifty guineas, and a dagger. The Irish also provided the prisoners with a supply of pickled beef, turkeys, coffee, tea, sugar, chocolate, whiskey, gin, and an assortment of fine wines.

Upon returning to his ship, Captain Symonds was enraged to discover that the Irishmen, whom he considered to be little better than rebels themselves, had been allowed to board the *Solebay* in the first place. He got really mad when he realized the extent of their generosity and that his prisoners now had supplies superior to his own. Symonds fixed the situation by immediately confiscating all the gifts except for the clothing, but Ethan had foreseen such a move and had hidden the dagger, some wine, and two gallons of whiskey. More Irishmen tried to visit the prisoners with gifts while the *Solebay* was anchored at Cork, but Symonds wouldn't allow them aboard.

About forty-five ships were in the fleet that set sail from Cork on February 12, 1776. Some of the prisoners were transferred to different vessels, although Ethan remained aboard the *Solebay*. The fleet hit another bad storm and was forced to put in at Madeira, but eventually it crossed the Atlantic and arrived at Cape Fear, North Carolina, on May 3. Ethan realized that if the British intended to murder him at sea, they would surely have done so before then, so he was somewhat encouraged. Despite the fact that he was still a captive, his future seemed a little brighter because he was back in America. The British half-expected Ethan to try to escape while they were anchored beside the American coast, so they kept him closely guarded. A prisoner named Peter Noble was able to jump off a different ship and swim several miles to freedom. Noble spread the news that the captives had been brought back, and knowledge of Ethan's whereabouts eventually filtered back to New England. The Allen family was relieved to hear that Ethan was alive and back in America, and they began to hope for his release.

The British fleet split up, with some of the ships departing to attack Charleston. Ethan and all the other remaining captives were loaded aboard the frigate *Mercury*, which was commanded by Captain James Montague, whom Ethan considered to be even meaner than Symonds. In early June, the *Mercury* sailed north and anchored off New York. Ethan was surprised to see a couple of his old enemies come aboard:

New York's Governor Tryon and former Attorney General Kempe, who were now apparently consorting with the British. Ethan was not able to hear the Yorkers' discussion with Montague, but he later concluded that they had had no kind words for him, because Montague's treatment of the prisoners suddenly became even harsher.

The *Mercury* continued north to the harbor at Halifax, in Canada. Ethan's outlook was brightened by being so close to home. But his physical condition did not match his optimism. The sailors and prisoners on the *Mercury* suffered from scurvy, a dreaded disease that causes soft gums, loosened teeth, and bleeding tissues. Scurvy is caused by a lack of vitamin C, and it is fatal if untreated. The crew was taken into Halifax for medical treatment, while the prisoners went untreated. They were transferred to a sloop in the middle of the harbor with no medical supplies and very little food. The only human contact that the prisoners were allowed was with their guards, some of whom were shocked by the mistreatment and did what they could to alleviate the suffering. A surgeon's mate managed to smuggle aboard a large vial of "smart drops" (now known as vitamin C) and gave the vial to Ethan, who doled it out to those with the worst cases of scurvy. There was not enough vitamin C to treat everyone, but it probably saved the lives of several prisoners.

One day a few Indians canoed near the sloop, and the miserable prisoners could see that the Indians had some fresh strawberries. One of the sick captives gave the natives everything he had in exchange for two quarts of the strawberries. It is unlikely that the poor prisoner had much to trade, but anytime a person spends everything they have, it is a major transaction. Still, it was a good deal for the prisoner, because the strawberries practically cured him.

Ethan wrote several letters to the ship's commander, complaining about the inhumane conditions on the sloop. The hard-hearted fellow responded by ordering his men not to deliver such letters in the future. Some of the guards onboard were sickened by the lack of basic decency and tried to help by smuggling ashore letters from Ethan. Eventually, Ethan was able to get word to the Connecticut legislature about the predicament, prompting his brother Levi and some other Connecticut citizens to open negotiations for Ethan's release through an exchange of prisoners. Another of Ethan's smuggled letters reached Governor Arbuthnot of Halifax, who dispatched a surgeon to the sloop to see if accounts of the conditions there were true. When the royal governor's surgeon informed him that the miserable conditions had not been exaggerated, Arbuthnot ordered the sick prisoners moved ashore to a city jail, where they received medical treatment. The humane governor also saw to it that the prisoners' diet improved and included fresh vegetables.

Although the Halifax jail was an improvement over the sloop, conditions were still unpleasant. Ethan was put into a large cell that was crowded with more than twenty captives and a couple of waste tubs. His constant appeals to the authorities to move the sickest of the prisoners to hospitals were ignored, and they spent the entire summer of 1776 in the cell. In October, Ethan and the other prisoners from the Montreal expedition were finally moved to the frigate *Lark,* which sailed for New York under the command of Captain Smith.

Ethan anticipated further harassment when he was summoned to the quarterdeck on October 12, assuming that Captain Smith would be as spiteful as most of the other British commanders. Ethan was pleasantly surprised to be greeted as an officer and a gentleman, and he was invited to dinner at the captain's table that night. Captain Smith allotted each prisoner a small, canvas-walled room between decks and fed them well.

Ethan took most of his meals in the gun room with a few other prisoners of gentleman status. One of these prisoners, a Captain Burk, had learned that the ship was transporting 35,000 pounds of sterling silver and that the crew that manned it had mutinous inclinations. Burk suggested that the prisoners join forces with the crew to seize the *Lark*, execute Captain Smith, and place his officers in chains. Ethan firmly rejected the idea of murdering the only commander who had treated him humanely during his captivity, and he even vowed to fight on the side of Captain Smith if the mutiny actually occurred. Ethan offered to forget about the proposal if it wasn't acted upon, however, and Burk abandoned the idea.

12

◆

Ethan on Parole

THE LAST VOYAGE OF ETHAN ALLEN'S CAPTIVITY ended in October
1776, when the *Lark* anchored at New York City. Ethan and
three of his officers were released on parole in the city, while
the rest of the prisoners were confined in a dirty old church
that had been converted into a prison and packed full. Ethan
and the three officers took an oath to remain within the city,
and since Ethan was a man of his word, he resisted the
temptation to flee to New England. Hungry, poor, sickly, and
thin, Ethan somehow managed to endure the winter of 1776,
the most discouraging time of the American Revolution. The
rebel forces were cold, underfed, and badly in need of a victory. Ethan slowly nursed himself back to health and spent
his time composing letters to the British commander. He described the horrible conditions in the converted church and
the high mortality rate of the prisoners and pleaded for improved treatment of his men.

One day a British officer greeted Ethan and brought him

an offer from General Howe. The British were prepared to give Ethan a colonel's commission to command a Tory detachment and serve under General John Burgoyne, fighting against the American rebels. The proposition included guineas (gold coins), a uniform, provisions, and a trip to England to meet with the king. All this and an enormous parcel of land in either the Grants or Connecticut would be granted to him after he helped Burgoyne recapture Fort Ticonderoga and conclude the war. Ethan declined, noting that the devil had once made a similar invitation to Jesus Christ by offering land that he didn't own.

Ethan's parole conditions were altered in January 1777. He and some of the other prisoners were allowed to relocate to the western end of Long Island, where Ethan found comfortable accommodations with a Dutch farmer in New Lots. Ira and Heman arranged to send money to Ethan, who also received eight pounds of back pay for his military service, two pounds from Jonas Fay, and thirty-five pounds from his brother Levi. Ethan suddenly could afford basic necessities and even a few luxuries. The parolees were allowed to move about freely during the daytime as long as they were back in their quarters at night, so they gathered in the taverns during the daytime, and Ethan entertained them with tales of his adventures.

It was not long before the tedium of his daily routine began to wear on Ethan. He was a man of action and got bored quickly, and his mood became even bleaker when he received a letter from Heman with the news that Joseph, Ethan's only son, had died from smallpox. Ethan became very depressed, and he was increasingly frustrated and impatient as his parole dragged on.

Significant events were occurring back in the Grants while Ethan fretted on Long Island. Ira's persistent efforts resulted in a convention on January 15, 1777, when delegates from twenty-two towns voted to create a new state in the Grants called New Connecticut. They originally intended to join the United States, but Congress rejected the proposed state. Refusing to admit defeat, a committee composed of Jonas Fay, Heman Allen, and Thomas Chittenden met with a philosopher named Dr. Thomas Young, who suggested that they form a separate republic, independent of any outside power. Young also suggested that they call the new republic Vermont, derived from the French words for "green mountains." Vermont was officially founded on June 4, 1777, in Windsor, when seventy-two delegates voted to form an independent republic by that name. They also voted to try to get delegates seated in the Continental Congress, to appoint public officials to replace the New York administrators, and to form a Committee of Safety.

In another important event that summer, General Burgoyne recaptured Fort Ticonderoga in July. Burgoyne dragged cannon to the top of a nearby hill that the Americans had considered too steep to fortify. With the British artillery overlooking their position, the Americans had little choice but to abandon the fort, and most of the retreating rebels followed the road leading toward Hubbardton and Castleton that Ira Allen and Remember Baker had constructed years before. Seth Warner and the Green Mountain Boys fought bravely at the Battle of Hubbardton when the British overtook them the following morning, and their valiant rearguard defense saved the retreating garrison from Fort Ticonderoga.

This news from the north made Ethan even more restless. Vermont's constitution was the first in the colonies to prohibit slavery, and it gave every man over the age of twenty-one a vote. Ethan must have been inspired to hear about that, but most of the news was bad. General Burgoyne announced that all Vermonters who failed to cooperate with the British would be killed and their property would be seized. Seventy-five percent of the settlers west of the Green Mountains chose to evacuate the area rather than remain under British domination.

The Americans earned a tremendous victory over General Burgoyne at the Battle of Bennington in August 1777, thanks to Seth Warner, Heman Allen, and the Green Mountain Boys. Ethan must have been thrilled by the news and yet irritated by his own enforced inactivity at such a momentous time. He began to violate his parole. Although he made no attempt to escape, Ethan repeatedly left Long Island to visit taverns and public rooms in Manhattan. The British authorities arrested him for parole violation and threw him into the provost jail in New York City on August 25.

According to his letters, Ethan almost preferred jail to the frustrations of parole, but he still seethed at his own futility as the war was waged without him. He was unable to spend the money that Levi sent him while he was in jail, so he spent his time learning French and writing long letters. He spent more than eight months in the guarded cell in New York.

Finally, in May 1778, Ethan was escorted to a sloop where he was wined and dined for two days and then released in a prisoner exchange. The fine treatment Ethan received during his last two days of captivity did not alter his resentment at his earlier treatment, and he promised the British that he would do his best to see that British prisoners also had to endure harsh treatment. After nearly three years of captivity, Ethan was finally exchanged for Colonel Archibald Campbell, and he received a hero's welcome at Elizabeth, New Jersey.

13

♦

A Hero's Welcome

FREE AT LAST, Ethan traveled to Valley Forge to meet with General George Washington, who recommended that Congress issue Ethan a commission in the army. From Valley Forge, where the Continental troops were trying to recover from the brutal winter, Ethan wrote a letter to Congress, thanking them for securing his freedom with the prisoner exchange. He described the terrible treatment he had endured as a prisoner and offered to be of service in some capacity.

Ethan left Valley Forge in the company of General Horatio Gates, who was traveling to his command in the north. Ethan and Gates got along very well, discussing philosophy and the fine points of real estate speculation as they rode to Fishkill, where they parted on friendly terms. Ethan continued on to Salisbury, where he learned that his brother Heman had died the week before from complications stemming from exposure that he had suffered at the Battle of Bennington.

Ethan was reunited with his wife and children in Sunderland. His three daughters, Loraine, Lucy, and Mary Ann, hardly recognized their famous father, who had been absent from their young lives for years. Ethan had seldom gotten along well with his wife Mary, and apparently their years of separation did not help that situation, because he left after two days.

While Ethan was attending a Council of Vermont session in Arlington, he received good news from George Washington: Congress had granted Ethan a commission as a brevet colonel in the army and awarded him back pay as a lieutenant colonel for the time he had spent in captivity.

Around this time, two young girls became lost in the Green Mountains, and their father, Eldad Taylor, organized a search party. About a hundred men searched for a few days with no success, and by midafternoon of the third day, many of the men were losing interest in the quest. They doubted that the girls would ever be found, and most of them wanted to quit the hunt. Ethan stepped forward to address the crowd of tired men, his huge frame towering over them all. He gave one of his rousing speeches, assuring the men that they would indeed find the girls and that he would continue the search all by himself if necessary. The men were sufficiently moved by his words to resume their search, and the two girls were rescued shortly afterward, further enhancing Ethan's reputation as a Green Mountain hero.

Ethan went with his brother Ira to the June session of the Vermont Assembly in Bennington, where people waved and cheered and greeted them with a hero's welcome as they came into town. Bennington was crowded with people eager not only to welcome Ethan home but to attend the Vermont Assembly meeting, and the Catamount Tavern did a lively business in whiskey, sherry flip, and rum punch. The celebrating militiamen dragged three old cannon onto a nearby hill and fired off three rounds in a salute to Colonel Allen. The following morning an enthusiastic patriot named Colonel Sam Herrick dressed up in his uniform and ordered the cannon fired fourteen times—one for each of the thirteen states in the Union and the final shot for Vermont.

Ethan remained in Bennington and rented a house near the center of town, only a short walk from the Catamount Tavern. He apparently had accepted the fact that he was incompatible with Mary—they had almost nothing in common and couldn't bear to live together in the same house, so Ethan elected to live alone.

The Republic of Vermont had been funding its government by selling off the land and property of Tories—people who were loyal to the king and opposed to the American Revolution—who had left the area and moved to areas controlled by the British. This system worked well for a while, but when the estates of the departed Tories had all been sold, Vermont was faced with the unpopular prospect of having to tax its citizens. Ethan suggested to the Vermont Assembly that the confiscation plan be expanded to include the property of Tories who were still residing within Vermont. His idea went over so well that he was appointed head judge on the Bennington board of confiscation. Ethan appointed the four additional judges, who were all approved by the legislature. He decided that those whose estates could be confiscated should include Yorker sympathizers and any enemies of the Republic of Vermont or the Green Mountain Boys.

Ethan and his men captured several of their adversaries and put them on trial. Some of the prisoners took an oath of allegiance and were released after they had paid for the cost of their trial, but eight who were deemed to be Yorkers as well as Tories were sentenced to banishment and relieved of their property. Ethan sent the eight banished prisoners to General John Stark in Albany and forwarded a letter to General Gates requesting that the prisoners be herded into the British lines. New York's Governor Clinton angrily demanded that Stark release the prisoners, whom Clinton believed to be loyal Yorkers and not Tories at all. Stark paid no heed to Clinton's demands and sent the prisoners on to Gates, who was about to follow his old traveling companion's advice and push the prisoners into the enemy lines when General George Washington intervened. Washington ordered the eight men sent to prison at West Point, much to the delight of the Vermonters and the disgust of the Yorkers.

During the summer of 1778, Governor Clinton tried to appease some of the Green Mountain settlers by offering to accept the patents of the original New Hampshire Grants as valid, as long as the New York claims were also accepted. This settlement would have left the Allen family, Thomas Chittenden, and many other Vermonters without any real estate, so it was rejected. Ethan responded to Clinton's ploy by writing propaganda that described the New York legislators as wicked people who were trying to cheat brave, patriotic Vermonters.

14

♦

Greater Vermont

WHILE RELATIONS WITH NEW YORK remained strained, Vermont's relationship with its neighbor to the east, New Hampshire, was also uneasy. The independent Republic of Vermont was very appealing to settlers because it offered a vote to every man and had managed to function without taxing its citizens. Sixteen towns on the New Hampshire side of the Connecticut River were so impressed with the fledgling republic that they offered to merge with Vermont. The threat of losing sixteen of their towns angered the New Hampshire authorities, who complained to Congress. Ethan Allen went to a session of Congress to meet with the New Hampshire delegates, however, and he persuaded them to retract their complaint until the next session of the Vermont Assembly, when (he assured them) the situation would be addressed. Then Ethan convinced Congress to pledge that Vermont would be accepted as a state if the sixteen towns were disowned and returned to New Hampshire.

Ethan then convinced the Vermont Assembly to omit the sixteen New Hampshire towns that wanted to join Vermont. Afterward he went back to Congress with the news that Vermont had voted to honor New Hampshire's border. But the sixteen towns in question were very disappointed that they could not join Vermont and informed Congress that they had no intention of returning to New Hampshire. If they were not allowed to join Vermont, they would form their own independent state. This threat to follow in Vermont's footsteps as an independent republic did not go over well in Congress, and certainly did nothing to improve Vermont's own status there. Congress did not honor its previous private agreement to admit Vermont as a state once the sixteen towns were rejected, electing to table the idea for further study instead.

Ethan performed these and many other important negotiations in an unofficial capacity. Although he had been elected to the Vermont Assembly, he refused to take the oath that was mandatory before assuming office. The oath required the declaration of faith in the Protestant religion, among other things. Ethan did believe in a Creator, in a way, referring to it as "nature," but he disputed the teachings of all organized religions and the clergy who preached them, so he wouldn't take any oath that supported religion. He attended every session of the Vermont Assembly anyway, however, and he was frequently named to serve in influential positions.

Ethan managed to find enough spare time from his duties as a statesman to complete what would become his most successful essay. *A Narrative of Colonel Ethan Allen's Captivity* was first published in 1779. It sold for ten paper dollars and soon became a best seller. Eight editions were published within two years, and at least nineteen editions were printed over a span of seventy-five years. In the essay Ethan mixed vivid descriptions of the awful treatment of war prisoners with ideas and thoughts about the world. The following quote from the narrative is about politics: "Virtue, wisdom, and policy, are in a national sense always connected with power, or in other words, power is their offspring, and such power as is not directed by virtue, wisdom, and policy, never fails to finally destroy itself as yours has done." Ethan's punctuation and style might be a bit old-fashioned, but his thoughts are still worthwhile.

In February 1779, the Vermont Assembly passed legislation authorizing the creation of a militia. An officer was assigned to each district and given the authority to draft men who lived inside his district. Any man who didn't want to serve had the option of paying eighteen pounds, which was then used to hire someone else to serve in his place. If a man who had been drafted refused to either serve or pay the substitute fee, the officer was authorized to seize and sell enough of the man's property to raise the eighteen pounds.

New York's Governor Clinton was worried by the prospect of a strong, organized militia in Vermont. Clinton was deeply opposed to Vermont independence because he owned New York grants that covered vast areas of the disputed land. His grants would be worthless if Vermont remained strong and independent, so he used his influence to stir up Yorker sentiment in Vermont, particularly in the area east of the Green Mountains. Encouraged by the New York authorities, a group of men from Putney resisted serving in the Vermont militia or paying the substitute fee. The officer in charge of the Putney district tried peaceful persuasion to get them to comply, but when that effort produced no results, he resorted to confiscation and seized two cows that he intended to sell to raise the eighteen pounds. On the day of the sale, however, a mob of more than a hundred men with Yorker sympathies gathered and prevented the sale, forcibly returning the cows to the draft dodgers.

The militia officer rode with news of these events to the Vermont Assembly, which spent some time discussing what would be an appropriate response. Meanwhile, Yorkers, Tories, and other enemies of the Republic of Vermont gathered in Brattleboro to compose a letter to Governor Clinton. They asked for New York troops to protect them from the "outlaw" republic. Clinton, delighted by this development, began preparations to send troops to aid the Yorker sympathizers.

The Vermont authorities considered the actions of the group in Brattleboro to be treasonous, however, and they asked Colonel Ethan Allen to handle the situation. Ethan was more than equal to the task; rallying his men with his cry that they were "going on a big wolf hunt," he assembled about a hundred Green Mountain Boys within a few days.

Ethan and his gang captured about forty of the most outspoken Yorkers and locked them up in the Westminster jail. In the process they confiscated a large stockpile of gunpowder and weapons and posted a detachment of alert sentries around the jail and courthouse. Ethan would have preferred to whip the Yorkers and banish them from Vermont, but his brother Ira had a better idea. He persuaded Judge Moses Robinson merely to fine those prisoners who were found guilty a small sum plus the cost of the trial. The convicted men were naturally quick to agree to the mild sentence. By doing so, however, they acknowledged the authority of the Republic of Vermont, which was what Ira had wanted them to do.

When he heard about the Westminster trials, Governor Clinton informed Congress that he intended to send a thousand New York militia troops to shatter the Republic of Vermont once and for all. With this goal in mind, Clinton wrote to General Washington and asked him to return the six cannon that New York had loaned the Continental Army. Washington was busy fighting the war against the British at the time, however, and the war was progressing poorly for the Americans. So the Continental Congress was too busy to deal with the issue of New York versus Vermont.

In Windsor the Assembly elected Ethan Allen commander of the Vermont militia with a rank of brigadier general. It also voted to pay the Green Mountain Boys who had volunteered to ride with Ethan to capture the Yorkers. But the best legislation of that session was a move masterminded by Ira Allen and Thomas Chittenden—a general pardon for past crimes by Yorker supporters. This pardon eliminated many potential enemies while creating many allies for the young republic.

Ethan's next pamphlet was the first to be printed in Vermont, and it was full of the usual propaganda about the rich, evil Yorkers trying to take advantage of the poor, honest Vermonters. Ira roamed far and wide to distribute the pamphlets to the legislatures in Maryland, New Jersey, Delaware, and Pennsylvania.

Congress demanded that Vermont stop trying to assert its independence until February 1780, when it—Congress— would settle the issue of Vermont. Most of the Vermont Assembly wanted to go along with the wishes of Congress, but Ethan wouldn't hear of it. He was still furious with Congress for failing to grant Vermont statehood after Vermont agreed to give up the sixteen New Hampshire towns. It took him five days of goading, but he finally persuaded the Assembly to pass a vote affirming Vermont's right to independence.

Ethan traveled to Massachusetts, where he discovered that New York, New Hampshire, and Massachusetts were all scheming to split Vermont's lands between them. This information inspired Ethan to write another pamphlet, co-written by Jonas Fay, that maintained that Vermont was an independent state, answerable only to heaven above and able to use armed resistance if necessary.

Congress cut off all military supplies to Vermont in February 1780, a drastic move considering that approximately three hundred Green Mountain Boys serving under Ethan Allen were the only obstacle between the struggling Continental Army and the British in Canada. Ethan dashed down to Connecticut and Massachusetts to personally purchase over five thousand pounds of gunpowder and lead for his Green Mountain Boys, and the Vermont Council passed legislation that prohibited the exportation of any wheat, flour, pork, or other supplies out of Vermont. The upstart republic braced itself to stand alone and even wage war against the United States if it proved unavoidable. Governor Chittenden and the Vermont Council wrote to Congress and threatened to make a separate peace with the British. They maintained that they were dedicated to remaining an independent state and pointed out that the United States should not expect Vermont to protect their northern boundary unless the republic was granted recognition. Congress was unmoved, however, and it left Vermont to its own defenses.

The British authorities soon contacted Vermont officials with plans for peace. The Vermont Assembly was not ready to rejoin the British Empire, but it did not want ten thousand British soldiers to pour into Vermont, either. To stall for time, the Assembly asked for an exchange of prisoners. The British agreed to refrain from attacking Vermont or northern New York during the exchange negotiations, which gained Vermont a little much-needed breathing room. Meanwhile, the British offered to make Vermont an independent province of Canada and to grant Ethan Allen command of a regiment and other personal concessions. This idea offended Ethan, who proclaimed that he would have nothing to do with any plan to sell his country for personal gain.

Realizing that stalling was his best tactic at that time,

Ethan milked the prisoner exchange negotiations for all they were worth. He claimed that he needed time to inform the Vermont citizens about the shortcomings of the Continental Congress and the merits of the British, and he agreed to disband the Vermont militia if the British withdrew their troops from the area. These negotiations could be interpreted as treason against the Americans, and there is little doubt that the Vermont leaders were guilty of treason against both the Continental Congress and the King of England. On the other hand, both of these governments had treated them badly. Congress had repeatedly refused to recognize Vermont as a separate state and had abandoned Vermont at a time when hostile troops were massing on her borders. The king's mismanagement had caused the land dispute with New York. It is understandable—perhaps even commendable—that the Green Mountain Boys were loyal to Vermont alone.

As part of the truce agreement between England and Vermont, Ethan dissolved the militia and resigned his command. The Assembly granted the town of East Haven to Ethan and his colleagues in reward for their services. Apparently the plan was to force Congress to come to a decision in support of either Vermont or New York. If Vermont got the nod, it would become a state. If not, it would become a Canadian province.

Congress still hadn't reached a decision about Vermont by November 1780, and many Congressional delegates were getting angry and anxious about the situation. The Continental Army tried to purchase provisions from Vermont, but the Vermont leaders would not sell to the army unless they were officially recognized. The Congressional delegates from Connecticut and Rhode Island began to argue on behalf of Vermont before the end of the year, and in early 1781 the New York Senate approved Vermont's independence. The House

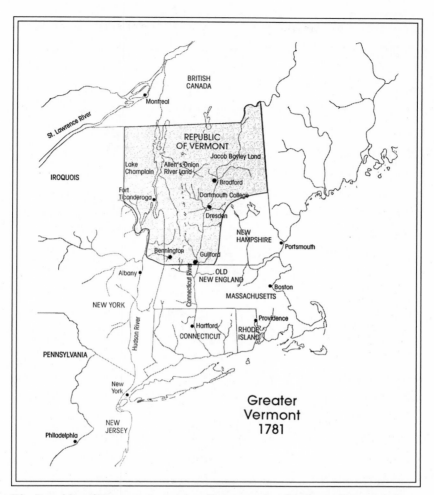

BRITISH
CANADA

Montreal

St. Lawrence River

REPUBLIC
OF VERMONT

Jacob Bayley Land

IROQUOIS

Lake
Champlain

Allen's Onion
River Land

Bradford

Fort
Ticonderoga

Dartmouth College

Dresden

NEW
HAMPSHIRE

Portsmouth

Bennington

Guilford

Albany

OLD
NEW ENGLAND

Boston

Connecticut River

MASSACHUSETTS

NEW YORK

Hudson River

Hartford

CONNECTICUT

RHODE
ISLAND

Providence

PENNSYLVANIA

New
York

NEW
JERSEY

Philadelphia

**Greater
Vermont
1781**

The Republic of Vermont was very well managed and in better financial shape than the infant United States in the early 1780s. Many towns in both New Hampshire and New York voted to join Vermont, and "Greater Vermont" grew to include large parts of eastern New York and western New Hampshire. Vermont later agreed to give up the territory in exchange for statehood, but Congress still wouldn't admit it into the Union. (Map by Michael Badamo)

appeared on the verge of recognizing Vermont, too, but Governor Clinton (whose personal fortune was at stake) intervened, threatening to dismiss the legislature rather than allow it to give up New York's claim to Vermont.

The Vermont Assembly's truce with the British encompassed not only Vermont but a strip of land west of Vermont that extended to the Hudson River, known as "the oblong" because of its shape. The New York citizens living in this eighty-by-twenty mile area were grateful to be included in the truce, and they were so impressed by the Green Mountain Republic that they asked to join Vermont. Ethan encouraged this idea, figuring that it could only help Vermont's bargaining position to increase her size and strength. With that in mind, Ira also revived the possibility of the sixteen New Hampshire towns joining Vermont. The discussions about acquiring land from New York and New Hampshire may only have been bargaining ploys, but in 1781 "Greater Vermont" (as Ethan began calling it) stretched from the Hudson River across the Connecticut River and deep into New Hampshire. The citizens of the oblong and the sixteen New Hampshire towns were perfectly serious about wanting to unite with the little republic, and town by town they voted to join Greater Vermont.

In the spring of 1781, Ira Allen and Joseph Fay, Dr. Jonas Fay's brother, met with the British at Skenesborough to exchange prisoners. The British wanted Vermont to commit to becoming a Canadian province, but Ira stalled, claiming that many Vermonters needed more time to decide. He thereby managed to prolong the truce. Then he went to Bennington for a meeting of the Vermont Assembly that included new towns from New York and New Hampshire. Vermont was uncertain which way to jump, especially since the French had entered the war on the side of the Americans, giving General Washington a real shot at victory. The British kept asking Vermont to join Canada as a province, but Vermont delayed, trying to put off making a decision until it became obvious who would win the war. The surrender of Cornwallis at Yorktown on October 19, 1781, should have convinced Vermont to join the United States, but when Congress offered Vermont a position in the union if it disowned the oblong and the New Hampshire towns, Vermont rejected the offer, apparently still uncertain about the outcome of the war.

Vermont's old enemy Governor Clinton called for an invasion of the republic in December, so Ethan rallied some of the Green Mountain Boys, and they dragged a small cannon to the oblong. Governor Clinton sent two hundred New York militiamen to the area, and Governor Chittenden dispatched about the same number of Green Mountain Boys to the Walloomsac (sometimes spelled Wallumscaik) River. The enemy forces faced off from opposite banks of the river and a few minor altercations occurred, but no serious engagement took place. Ethan soon received a large group of reinforcements, and he paraded them up and down the riverbank to the sounds of marching music and cannon fire, inspiring the Yorkers to slink away in retreat.

The idea of becoming a Canadian province was losing its appeal because of the reduced military strength of the British, so Ira Allen and Jonas Fay went to Philadelphia to petition Congress again for Vermont statehood. Meanwhile, Governor Chittenden received a letter from George Washington saying that Vermont would be accepted as an independent state if it gave up the new lands. Ira and Ethan opposed this concession, but they were unable to prevent the Vermont Assembly from voting to give up the New Hampshire towns and the oblong. But Congress once again didn't hold up its end of the bargain—it refused to seat the Vermont delegates. Vermont had lost the oblong and the New Hampshire towns, establishing its boundaries as they are today, but it had not gained statehood. When Congress actually demanded that Vermont pay back all of the people who had been banished or had their property seized, Chittenden and the Council angrily replied that Congress had no authority over Vermont's internal legal business. Most Vermont citizens were thoroughly disgusted with Congress for not honoring its offer of statehood and for trying to interfere with Vermont's affairs. Ethan was roaring mad, and he demanded that Vermont reject the United States and remain an independent republic. The Republic of Vermont was on her own.

15

---◆---

Ethan's Final Days

In 1782, Ethan completed his most controversial manuscript, a philosophical book that harshly criticized organized religion. *Reason the Only Oracle of Man* was constructed from notes that Ethan had written years earlier in Salisbury with Dr. Thomas Young, the man who had later suggested that the new republic be named Vermont instead of New Connecticut. These notes had been tucked away among Dr. Young's possessions and forgotten. Then Dr. Young passed away, and they came into Ethan's possession. He revised the old jottings into a manuscript that he thought was publishable, but this sentiment was not shared by the printers in Hartford who had printed most of Ethan's political pamphlets. They were shocked by the blasphemous work and had no desire to be associated with it in any way. On the other hand, Ethan was a respected writer with whom they had been doing business for quite some time, and they didn't want to offend him.

They tried to persuade him to abandon the project, but he insisted that it must be printed.

While this haggling was going on, Ethan received word that he was needed back home to quell a Yorker uprising. Governor Clinton had once again stoked Yorker sympathy in eastern Vermont, and he had sent the citizens of Guilford a supply of ammunition that they were using to perform military drills while preparing to defy Vermont authority. Forty of these Yorkers from Guilford had prevented a Vermont sheriff from carrying out a written order from the state; the sheriff had appealed to the Vermont Council, which had sent for Ethan.

Ethan was upset that Vermont had conceded all the extra land of Greater Vermont—he believed that Vermont had shown weakness. Determined to prove to New York and New Hampshire that Vermont had the strength at least to remain independent, he left his sensitive manuscript with the flustered printers in Hartford and returned to Vermont. He recruited two hundred Green Mountain Boys from the Bennington area and headed for Guilford. The situation there had grown worse—a Yorker sheriff named Tim Phelps had recently beaten a Vermont sheriff with a pitchfork handle. Ethan presented an imposing figure as he took the trail wearing a grand uniform, riding a big black horse, and armed with a gigantic sword.

Although he wanted to make a show of strength, Ethan preferred a bloodless victory, because he didn't want to give Congress any excuse to send the Continental Army into Vermont. Unfortunately, the mission started out poorly. Ethan sent Ira, in command of an advance guard of twenty men, into Guilford to arrest Phelps. They could not locate Phelps in town, so they headed back out to rejoin Ethan and the rest of the Green Mountain Boys. But Phelps and fifty Yorkers ambushed them before they reached Ethan, and Ira's group had to retreat into Guilford. Several Green Mountain Boys were hit by the initial volley of gunfire. Ethan stormed into Guilford and took control of the situation by thundering, "I, Ethan Allen, do declare that I will give no quarter to the man, woman, or child who shall oppose me, and unless the inhabitants of Guilford peacefully submit to the authority of Vermont, I swear that I will lay it as desolate as Sodom and Gomorrah, by God."

The townspeople of Guilford were shaken by these startling words, and the resolve to fight deserted them. Phelps was captured unharmed and dragged before Ethan while defiantly demanding that the Green Mountain Boys stop in the name of New York. Ethan drew his tremendous sword and slashed the hat from Phelps's head, quickly silencing the man without harming him.

Additional Green Mountain Boy volunteers arrived steadily, numbering more than four hundred by the time they strode into Guilford. They made several arrests in Guilford, Halifax, and Brattleboro without drawing any blood, then took their Yorker prisoners to Westminster for trial. Most of the prisoners received only a small fine or a short jail sentence, but six of them were banished from Vermont and their property was confiscated. When Congress was informed of these events, it condemned Vermont's actions, which further widened the gap between the United States and the Republic of Vermont.

The American Revolution ended in the spring of 1783. After the war was over, the British stopped trying to convince Vermont to join Canada because the move was no longer important to them. New York and Vermont continued to quarrel. When New York ships refused to carry Vermont goods, Ira Allen arranged to market Vermont products through Quebec. The Republic of Vermont thrived as timber and livestock were transported north to the French Canadians and traded for manufactured goods from England. Ethan's estranged wife Mary died that year, succumbing to tuberculosis before she reached fifty, and their daughter Loraine passed away a few months later. Ethan kept a low profile during this time of grief, avoiding the public eye to quietly focus on his writing, but he was drawn out of his shell to reopen the Onion River Company with Ira and Joseph Fay. The time was ripe to repopulate the empty lands of northern Vermont, which had been virtually abandoned due to the threat of Indians and British during the war. Vermont welcomed Tories and American deserters who had fled to Canada, as well as just about almost anyone else who was hardy enough to settle in the rugged wilderness.

Vermont real estate became valuable, and trading was brisk as settlers from Connecticut vied with British deserters and other prospective homesteaders for a piece of the little republic. Ira Allen became the largest landholder in Vermont, and all of the Allens, the Fays, and Thomas Chittenden bought and sold large amounts of real estate and made healthy profits. While Vermont was enjoying this boom of prosperity, the United States was not faring as well. Hampered by a large war debt, the United States was unable to pay soldiers for their service in the Continental Army, and a disorganized and ineffective Congress did little to improve the situation. It is not surprising that deserters from the Continental Army continued to come to Vermont, which had a financially solid and well-run government.

The Yorkers made one final attempt to impose their authority in Vermont. A group of armed Yorkers assaulted a Vermonter named Luke Knowlton in Newfane and hauled him off to Massachusetts. News of the attack reached Governor Chittenden, who knew, of course, that Ethan Allen was the man to solve the problem. Ethan, in turn, sent out the word for the Green Mountain Boys to gather at the Catamount Tavern. Excitement ran high as the troops anticipated another expedition under Ethan Allen, but they never had to perform their mission. The news that Ethan was rallying his men was enough to scare the Yorkers, and they released Luke Knowlton, who reappeared in Vermont unharmed.

The Yorkers were not much of a problem after that, but Ethan knew the value of presenting a strong image. He took a number of his Green Mountain Boys to Westminster during the winter of 1784 to make sure that Yorkers did not interfere with a meeting of the Vermont district court there. No confrontations with Yorkers took place in Westminster that winter, but there was a momentous meeting of a gentler nature—Ethan fell in love.

Fanny Montresor Buchanan was a very pretty, intelligent, twenty-four-year-old woman who had been married at the age of sixteen to a British officer who was later killed in the war. Fanny captured Ethan's heart, and the bold young widow returned Ethan's affection. Their courtship was brief. Legend has it that Ethan walked into the dining room where Fanny was having breakfast on February 9 and told her that the time had come for their marriage if it was going to happen, because he was leaving for Sunderland. Fanny replied that she just needed time to get her coat and she would be ready. Ethan's old friend Judge Robinson was having breakfast next door, and he married the couple then and there.

Fanny and Ethan piled her belongings into Ethan's sleigh and drove over the mountains to Sunderland, where they moved into a house that Ethan co-owned with Ira. Ethan's second marriage was a very good match. Although some of Sunderland's idle gossipers might have had a few unkind things to say about Ethan's spirited young wife, who played

REASON

THE ONLY

ORACLE OF MAN,

OR A

Compenduous System

OF

Natural RELIGION.

Alternately ADORNED with Confutations
of a variety of DOCTRINES
incompatible to it ;
Deduced from the most exalted Ideas which
we are able to form of the

DIVINE and Human

CHARACTERS,

AND FROM THE

Univerſe in General.

By Ethan Allen, *Eſq;*

===

BENNINGTON:
STATE OF VERMONT;
Printed *by* HASWELL & RUSSELL.
M,DCC,LXXXIV.

The publication of Reason the Only Oracle of Man *led to many problems for Ethan. It landed him in court for failure to pay his printing bills, and it inspired the anger of religious officials, who were very powerful at the time. (George Keiser photograph, courtesy of the Ethan Allen Homestead)* the guitar, wore fancy clothes, and was known to have an independent mind, Fanny and Ethan were happy together. Their first child, a daughter named Fanny, was born November 13.

Ethan devoted a lot of time to getting *Reason the Only Oracle of Man* published, but it was a difficult task because all the publishers were wary of the extremely controversial book. He finally convinced a Bennington printing press named Haswell and Russell to print fifteen hundred copies of the treatise in 1784 by agreeing to pay for them as they were printed. This was the first work published in America that disputed organized religion—it denounced both the Old and the New Testaments. The religious communities were outraged by the book, which was jokingly referred to as Allen's Bible. The book states that nature is God in action and harmony with nature is godliness; the creator of the universe is totally beyond the knowledge of mankind, it says, and weak humans invented God as a comforting power. Ethan believed that prayer was useless and maybe even rude because the power that rules the universe is guided by a perfect plan and it does not heed our prayers. Ethan advised his readers to shun prophets and preachers and to stop wasting money on clergymen. He suggested that they should spend it on alcoholic beverages instead, which would at least give them some return for their investment.

The priests and preachers whom the book criticized quickly mounted a strong counterattack. They gave long, hostile speeches about how Ethan was a wicked, swearing, drinking sinner who refused to acknowledge the existence of God and who was known to overindulge even on Sundays. Their crusade was effective among religious people, and the book unquestionably damaged Ethan's reputation. Sales were predictably slow—only two hundred of the fifteen hundred copies ever sold, and most of those were bought by ministers so they could read some of the evil passages while they condemned the work from their pulpits. Ethan had borrowed money to get the book published, and when it sold poorly, he had trouble repaying the loan—he was even hauled into court for failing to meet his payments. *Reason the Only Oracle of Man* was one of the two notable failures in Ethan's life; his first marriage was the other.

Ethan's marriage with Fanny was good, however, and despite his shortage of cash, he still owned lots of valuable real estate. He had acquired about 150 acres of good farmland near Burlington in 1778, and he decided to build a farm. When Ethan and Ira dissolved the Onion River Land Company, part of the deal was that Ethan's title to the Burlington farmland was confirmed. Ira also agreed to build Ethan a twenty-four by thirty-four-foot house, and to give Ethan a hundred pounds worth of supplies every year for seven years. When Ethan moved onto the farm, he bought adjacent lots, expanding the size of the farm to at least nine hundred acres. Fanny was pregnant again and Ethan didn't want to put her through too much stress, so he initially traveled alone to the new home on the Onion River, making the place comfortable before he returned to Sunderland for Fanny, baby Fanny, and his daughters from his first marriage. They made the trip north to Burlington with a large number of home supplies and a pair of hired hands whom Ethan had hired to help run the farm.

A son was born to Ethan and Fanny on November 24, 1787, and they named him Hannibal. The farm now totaled fourteen hundred acres of good river bottom land, and the future seemed bright. Ethan enjoyed a few years of closeness with his brothers Ira and Levi. Ira was very busy, involved in trading with Canada, mining, farming, real estate speculation, fur trading, and any other potentially prosperous occupations. Levi sold livestock and lumber in Canada, managing the northern end of Ira's businesses. Ethan worked on the farm and entertained people with his wonderful stories, but he missed philosophy, and he started to write another book.

Ethan never forgave Congress for not holding up its end of the deal to make Vermont a state in exchange for giving up the additional lands of Greater Vermont, and he wanted Vermont to remain an independent republic. Congress, for its part, was not fond of Vermont, and it despised the Allen family in general and Ethan in particular. The delegates from New York and New Hampshire were particularly bitter over the old land dispute, and Vermont and the United States remained aloof.

The weather was bad in 1788, causing the hay and grain crops in Vermont to be small. Vermont farmers felt the effects of the poor growing season in early 1789, when the Vermont Council prohibited the export of corn and wheat in order to avoid famine. Ethan's hay crop was no bigger than his neighbors', so he was pleased to learn that his cousin Ebenezer Allen had harvested a good crop of hay on South Hero Island. Ebenezer wrote Ethan to say that he was welcome to come and get a wagonload of hay, and Ethan and one of his hired men hitched up the team of oxen and headed across the frozen lake on February 11. The weather was typical for February in Vermont, and Ethan brought along a jug to raise his spirits during the long, cold ride and loading of hay in the inclement weather.

News got out that Ethan was visiting the island, and about twenty Green Mountain Boy veterans crowded around the fireplace at Ebenezer's house that night to tell tall tales about the good old days, washing the stories down with rum and hard cider. Ethan was in his element at such a gather-

Ethan Allen spent the last months of his life in this cabin on what is now the northern edge of the city of Burlington. He had a large farm and what is presumed to be a peaceful and happy home. He was bringing hay for the farm back from South Hero when he suffered what may have been a cerebral hemorrhage and died in February 1789. (Photograph by Harry Wicks, courtesy of the Ethan Allen Homestead)

ing and enjoyed himself, but he was up before daylight the following morning, heading home across the ice in the hay wagon with his hired hand in the biting wind. They were entering the mouth of the Onion River when the hired man noticed Ethan struggling wildly, suffering some kind of fit. Some historians speculate that Ethan suffered a cerebral hemorrhage—at any rate, he fell unconscious into the sleigh within a half hour. The hired hand covered Ethan with a blanket and kept driving toward the farm.

When the hired hand carried the still-unconscious Ethan into the farmhouse that afternoon, Fanny assumed that he had passed out from drinking and angrily ran to another part of the house. Ethan never regained consciousness. A doctor bled him, and although this questionable practice probably didn't help him, he almost certainly would not have recovered anyway. Ethan died at home on the afternoon of February 12, 1789.

The extent of the respect people felt for Ethan was shown by the hundreds who braved a blizzard to travel by sleigh to his funeral. One man named Major Goodrich actually snowshoed all the way from Vergennes to Ira's home near Burlington to attend the service on February 16. Ethan was given a soldier's funeral: sixteen squads of Green Mountain Boys marched to drumbeats across the ice of the Onion River, stopping now and then to fire a cannon, and Governor Chittenden was one of the pallbearers. The coffin was set into a frozen grave on the crest of a hill, crossed swords were placed on the coffin, then three musket volleys were fired in salute. The obituary in the *Gazette* praised Ethan as a great hero.

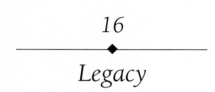

16

Legacy

Eᴛʜᴀɴ ᴀɴᴅ Fᴀɴɴʏ's ꜱᴇᴄᴏɴᴅ ꜱᴏɴ was born on October 24, 1789, and was named Ethan Alphonso Allen. Both Ethan Alphonso and his older brother Hannibal eventually attended the United States Military Academy at West Point, graduated as second lieutenants of artillery, and rose to the rank of captain.

A granite column was erected in 1858 as a monument near Ethan's gravesite, and a statue was mounted atop the column in 1871. Ethan was fifty-two years old when he suffered the attack on the hay wagon, and he left behind a sizable estate, which was settled for $69,823.36 in 1802 and divided among Fanny and the children from both of Ethan's marriages. Fanny later married for a third time, to a Dr. Jabez Penniman from Westminster. Ethan's daughter Fanny became a beloved nun, and the Fanny Allen Hospital in Winooski was eventually founded in her name.

Ethan had spent a lot of energy to keep Vermont an independent republic, but without his support the Republic of Vermont dissolved only two years after he died. Ira convinced the people who held the old New York land grants to settle for the sum of $30,000, which was a very good deal for Vermont. The Vermont delegates voted to join the United States in January 1791 by a margin of 105 to 2. With the old land dispute settled, there was no opposition in Congress to accepting Vermont as a state, and a unanimous vote with no debate granted Vermont full statehood on March 4, 1791.

Ethan's vision of an independent republic slipped away, but his legacy of independence endures in the people of Vermont today. He was a rambunctious, rowdy adventurer who was also a bold, resourceful thinker and a skilled military man. Vermont and America owe a debt of gratitude to this man who was so perfectly suited to the extraordinary events of his lifetime.

Chronology

Date	Ethan Allen	Vermont	North America
1737	EA was born in January.		
1749		Wentworth began granting charters.	
1762	EA married Mary Brownson.		
1763	EA & family moved to Salisbury.	The Treaty of Paris ended the French & Indian Wars.	France yieded all her NA holdings east of the Mississippi to Great Britain. Spain ceded Florida to Great Britian.
1765	EA & family moved to Northampton.	New York surveyors began measuring Grants homesteads without permission.	English colonials demonstrated against the Stamp Act.
1770	EA bought land in the Grants and was elected colonel-commandant of the military associaiton of the Grants men.		Five people were killed in the Boston Massacre.
1771	EA & Green Mountain Boys burned Yorker buildings in Rupert. A reward was offered for EA.	The Green Mountain Boys prevented the eviction of James Breakenridge by a NY sheriff. A price was put on the heads of several Green Mountain Boys.	
1773	The Onion River Company was formed.		The English tax on tea was protested by the Boston Tea Party.
1775	EA captured Fort Ticonderoga. EA attempted to capture Montreal, but was taken prisoner by the British. He was shipped to England in December.	The Westminster Massacre was the first bloodshed of the American Revolution.	The battles of Lexington and Concord were fought in April.
1776	EA was moved back to America, still a prisoner. He was paroled in October.	Benedict Arnold earned a costly delay at the Battle of Valcour.	The Declaration of Independence was signed on July 4th.

Chronology

Date	Ethan Allen	Vermont	North America
1777	EA was jailed by the British for parole violation.	Vermont declared herself an independent republic. The British won the Battle of Hubbardton but lost the Battle of Bennington.	The Continental Congress adopted the Stars and Stripes. Burgoyne surrendered at Sarasota.
1778	EA was released in May, exchanged for Colonel Archibald Campbell.	Vermont held her first general elections, electing Thomas Chittenden governor.	
1779	*A Narrative of Colonel Ethan Allen's Captivity* was published. EA was elected brigadier general in the Vermont Militia.		
1780		Vermont was involved in delicate negotiations with both the Continental Congress and the British.	
1781		Greater Vermont stretched from the Hudson River deep into New Hampshire.	General Cornwallis surrendered to George Washington at Yorktown.
1782	Mary Brownson Allen died.		
1784	EA married Fanny Montresor Buchanan in February; they had a daughter in November. *Reason the Only Oracle of Man* was published.	Five Vermont towns started a postal service.	
1787	EA and Fanny had a son named Hannibal.		
1789	EA died in February. A second son was born in October named Ethan Alphonso.	A commission was appointed to settle the Vermont-New York border dispute.	
1791		Vermont became the 14th State.	

Bibliography

Alderman, Clifford Lindsey. *Gathering Storm: The Story of the Green Mountain Boys.* J. Messner, 1970.

Allen, Ethan. *A Narrative of Colonel Ethan Allen's Captivity Containing his Voyages and Travels.* Vermont Heritage Press, 1988.

Allen, Ethan and Ira. *Collected Works by Ira Allen.* Chalidze Publications, 1992.

Bellesiles, Michael A. *Revolutionary Outlaws: Ethan Allen and the Struggle for Independence on the Early American Frontier.* University Press of Virginia, 1993.

Brown, Charles Walter. *Ethan Allen of Green Mountain Fame: A Hero of the Revolution.* M. A. Donohue & Co., 1902.

Brown, Slater. *Ethan Allen and the Green Mountain Boys.* Random House, 1956.

Clinton, Susan. *The Story of the Green Mountain Boys.* Children's Press, 1987.

De Morgan, John. *The Hero of Ticonderoga or Ethan Allen and his Green Mountain Boys.* David McKay, 1896.

De Puy, Henry Walter. *Ethan Allen and the Green Mountain Heroes of '76.* Phinney & Co., 1853.

Fraetas, Josiah A. *Ethan Allen* or *The King's Men: A Historical Novel.* W. H. Graham, 1846.

Hall, Henry. *Ethan Allen: The Robin Hood of Vermont.* D. Appleton & Co., 1892.

Heckerwinders, Gertrude. *Ethan Allen: Green Mountain Boy.* Bobbs Merrill, 1962.

Himelhoch, Myra. *The Allens in Early Vermont.* Star Printing and Publishing Co., Inc., 1967.

Holbrook, Stewart Hall. *America's Ethan Allen.* Houghton Mifflin Co., 1949.

Hoyt, Edwin Palmer. *The Damndest Yankees: Ethan Allen and his Clan.* Greene Press, 1976.

Jellison, Charles A. *Ethan Allen: Frontier Rebel.* Syracuse University Press, 1969.

Ripley, Sheldon N. *Ethan Allen: Green Mountain Hero.* Houghton Mifflin, 1961.

Sparks, Jared. *The Life of Colonel Ethan Allen.* C. Goodrich & Co., 1858.

Spargo, John. *Ethan Allen at Ticonderoga.* The Tuttle Co., 1926.

Victor, Orville James. *The Life and Times of Colonel Ethan Allen, the Hero of Ticonderoga.* Beadle & Adams, 1896.

Index